D1483391

CLUES
TO OUR FAMILY NAMES

What do they mean?   How did they begin?

by Lou Stein

RAMSBOTTOM
LONGBOTTOM
WINTERBOTTOM
RAGBOTTOM
SIDEBOTTOM
ROEBOTTOM
HIGGENBOTTOM

WESCOTT
ESCOTT
PRESCOTT
ENDICOTT
WALCOTT
NORCOTT
CAULDCOTT

HERITAGE BOOKS, INC.
1986

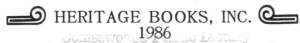

Published By

HERITAGE BOOKS, INC.
3602 Maureen Lane, Bowie, MD 20715

ISBN 1-55613-009-0

Dedicated to Ellie.

CONTENTS

PREFACE

Surnames in a phonebook are fossilized echoes of ancient voices of ancestors singling out each other in fields, castles, manor halls, monasteries, and medieval villages.

Surname comes from the medieval French *surnom* translating as "above-or-over name". Ancient French legal documents and records differentiated a particular Pierre and a particular Marie from other Pierres and Maries by enscribing a second name over a first name:

du <u>bois</u> (the woodcutter)
<u>Pierre</u>

la <u>blanc</u> (the blonde-haired one)
<u>Marie</u>

(Inherited family names in France became a national custom around 1200 A.D.)

The telephone directory, which came into our home with our first telephone when I was in high school, sparked my initial interest in surnames. I discovered words like *Upjohn*, *Leeper*, *Quint*, *Buggs*, *Coward*, *Goforth*, *Properjohn*, *Steptoe*, *Outhouse*, *Sinyard*, *Hogge*, *Belcher*, *Lawless*, *Pettibone*, *Popejoy*, *Mucklejohn*, and *Pigge*. And I wondered: Could these really be family names? What did they mean? How did they come into usage?

Thus began a lifetime of historical sleuthing which led me into collections of names.

Buggs is derived from: bogeyman.
Upjohn is derived from: John's son.
Coward is derived from: cow herder.
Goforth is derived from: the messenger.
Quint is derived from: fifth son.
Mucklejohn is derived from: Big John.
Properjohn is derived from: Robert, son of John.
Steptoe is derived from: walked on his toes.
Outhouse is derived from: lived beyond village limits.
Sinyard is derived from: monseigneur or lordship.
Hogge is derived from: slovenly one.
Belcher is derived from: beloved one.
Lawless is derived from: the outlaw.
Leeper is derived from: the dancer.
Pettibone is derived from: useless one.
Pigge is derived from: piglike one.
Popejoy is derived from: parrot face.

Bottom was a medieval location name for a deep valley, describing a wind-sheltered hollow for a residence or for sheep grazing. Thus a solitary homestead in a valley often became the address which identified an early ancestor:

Ramsbottom is derived from: ram grazing place or place of wild garlic, from the Old English ramm. (Not until I entered college did I learn, to my dismay, that *Ramsbottom* did not mean: south end of a ram facing north!)

Longbottom is derived from: narrow valley floor.

Winterbottom is derived from: winter-grazing hollow.

Sidebottom is derived from: very wide valley.

Ragbottom is derived from: site of many fungus plants.

Roebottom is derived from: water source for deer.

Higgenbottom is derived from: homestead of Higgens in a hollow.

Dale, *Vail*, *Dean*, *Dell*, or *Glen* were medieval regional variations for valley. *Bottom* was a preferred descriptive in northern England. Some later ancestors chose to camouflage *Bottom*, spelling it as *Botham*.

The suffix "cott" identified settlement ancestors:

Wescott lived in a cottage in the western part of the village.

Escott lived in a cottage in the eastern part of the village.

Endicott lived in an end cottage.

Prescott is derived from: priest's cottage.

Walcott identified the Welshman's cottage.

Norcott lived in a cottage in the northern part of the village.

Cauldcott lived in a cottage in the coldest or windiest part of the village.

The history of our English language is an archive of people spelling, pronouncing, and identifying names of things, places, neighbors, strangers, and occasional enemies.

For example: The Normans who invaded England in 1066 A.D. galloped through England's countryside on magnificent and well cared for horses. Norman marechals (marshalls) served as horse shoers and veterinarians to guard the health and well-being of these animals, second in importance only to the army's warriors.

The conquered Anglo-Saxons, forced to learn French and doing a bad job of it, soon corrupted *Mareschal* into *Marescal*. By 1200 A.D. the meaning of the word changed from that of care-taker for horses to *Marschal*, a charge d'affairs of military management for a king. In 1575 A.D., Shakespeare wrote it as *Marshal*. Today, a British military chief-of-staff is titled *Marshall* and an American *Marshal* is an official in a fire department or a government policeman in a federal court of law. Thus, the military importance of horses and *Marshalls* marched side-by-side with the development of nation and language in Great Britain and in the United States.

Clues To Our Family Names is not a dictionary. It is an informal history book. Its theme is to inform the reader about how our last names reflect and record the conditions of daily life in medieval Britain. Its pattern of emphasis continually reminds the reader that our surnames evolved alongside nine hundred years of growth of the English language.

There are more than one million surnames in America. If a reader's last name is not mentioned in this book, he or she may consult Chapter 7 on how to search efficently for the root and meaning of that surname.

I am familiar with Elsdon C. Smith's books on American surnames and I am greatly indebted to this outstanding scholar and notable fellow-member of the American Name Society.

Lou Stein

LIST OF ABBREVIATIONS

A.S.	Anglo-Saxon
Arab.	Arabian
Aus.	Austrian
Bulg.	Bulgarian
Czech.	Czechoslovakia
Dan.	Danish
Du.	Dutch
Finn.	Finnish
Fr.	French
Ger.	German
Heb.	Hebrew
Hung.	Hungarian
Ir.	Irish
Isr.	Israeli
Ital.	Italian
	Latin
Nor.	Norwegian
O. Da.	Old Danish
O. E.	Old English
O. Fr.	Old French
O. Nor.	Old Norwegian
Pol.	Polish
Port.	Portuguese
Rom.	Romanian
Rus.	Russian
Scan.	Scandinavian
Scot.	Scottish
Swed.	Swedish
Yugo.	Yugoslavia

CHAPTER 1

THEY HAD TO CALL US SOMETHING!

Many of us have last names that can be traced back
to the time of William the Conqueror's invasion of
Britain in 1066 A.D. Such names with origins in the
Middle Ages give us information about our ancestors
who lived in England, Ireland, Scotland, and Wales:

OCCUPATION – Some ancestors worked in castles,
towns, churches, the countryside, or in shops as
craftsman or tradesmen. (Clothmaking was an
important English industry in the Middle Ages and
produced such names as *Taylor*, *Dyer*, *Cutter*, *Fuller*, *Tucker*, *Walker*, *Woolman*, *Sheperd*, and
Draper).

PHYSICAL DESCRIPTION – Some family names
describe the physical appearances or qualities of our
long ago ancestors: *Byrd*, *Crane*, *Baines*, *Longfellow*, *Kennedy*, *Lemon*, *Merriman*, *Truman*, *Cruikshanks*, *Campbell*. Such names often originated as
nicknames.

ADDRESS – Some family names offer clues to the
places where people lived and worked: *Marsh*,
Groves, *Dale*, *Wood*, *Bourne(s)*, *Brook(s)*, *Wells*,
Meadows, *Fields*, *Waters*, *Hedges*, *Poole*, *Oak-
wood*, *Ford*, *Hartfield*, *Elmore*, *Riggs*, *Ridgeway*,
Shaw, *Heath* or *Muir*, and *Hill* or *Hillman*.

FIRST NAME OF A PARENT – A most common
surnaming custom before 1300 A.D. was to identify a

1

male by attaching a son's name to his father's name: John *Andrewson* (son of Andrew). Girls were often surnamed as Joan "Tomsdogther" and Ann "Willsdogther"; the "daughter" suffix disappeared when the female married. By 1300 A.D. most surnames had become permanent.

- NINE HUNDRED YEARS OF NAME-HISTORY -

English is the result of criss-crossing vocabulary trails made by seafarers and conquerors who came to Britain from Rome, Norway, Sweden, Denmark, Germany, and France. Their pursuit of spoils in Britain eventually established five trails of alien people intermingling five alien languages: the Celtic, Roman (Latin), Anglo-Saxon, Scandinavian, and French speech patterns.

LATIN TRAIL of WORDS

Celtic tribes from Europe overran Britain about 300 B.C. The disciplined Roman legions of Julius Caesar conquered the Celts in 55 B.C. and they named their new colony "Brittannia" (land of the Bretons).

The following British map names of today are word fossils from the Roman invasion of 55 B.C. "Chester" is from the Latin *castra* meaning "place of a walled encampment":

Chester	Gloucester
Colchester	Leicester
Dorchester	Worcester

CELTIC TRAIL of WORDS

-- The fur-clad dancers waved wolf tails above their heads, shouting joyfully as they circled a black rock monument located on the western shore of the Atlantic Ocean near Lough Swilly Bay in ancient Ireland. The

2

shouting diminished as the dancers turned to observe the setting sun. One by one the people sat, forming a half-circle. A tall and gaunt, blue-eyed druid priest, carrying a rawskin sack, appeared from behind this primitive, sacred rock site of worship. From his bag he drew a handful of mistletoe and large oak leaves, placing a mistletoe sprig on the fur cap of each male dancer and an oak leaf on the head of each female dancer. The priest then faced the assembled group and intoned a slow, dramatic complaint about the season's winter of extreme chill, rain, and storming winds:

Fuit co brath!
Is mo in donen ar cach;
Is obcach etrice an,
O cus is loch mor cod loch loun,
Abair nech acht fuit!

Cold till doom!
The storm is greater than ever;
Each furrow is a river,
And a full lake each ford,
None say aught but cold! --

By 400 A.D., strong-armed pirates in long sailboats manned by Angles, Saxons, Picts, or Jutes, looted and ravaged monasteries, gravesites, and grain storehouses throughout Brittania. Many of these Germanic tribes eventually settled in Brittania. After many tribal skirmishes, Anglo-Saxon military mastery subjugated most of Brittania. By 700 A.D. the Anglo-Saxon language was "the tongue of Angle-land". However, the Gaelic (Celtic) language still prevailed in isolated regions of Ireland, Manx, Wales, and Scotland.

Celtic names in today's Ireland:

3

mac Donald (domnhall, "dark-haired stranger")
mac Cormack (cormac, "the cartman")
mac Duffy (dubhshithe, "man of peace")
mac Sweeney (suibhne, "always merry")
mac Mahon (mathgam, "of bear strength")

(The Celts had no family names.)

ANGLO-SAXON TRAIL of WORDS

-- A tall and gaunt, blue-eyed minstrel gazed around at the one hundred knights seated at King Arthur's Round Table. The bard's harp rang through the hall and he boasted about a valorous, brave knight:

se god beold cniht libban strang hus an hyle

this good, bold knight lived in a strong house on a hill --

The Anglo-Saxons had no surnames. Examples of names in 515 A.D. include:

Breme (famed warrior)
Eofor (boar-ferocity)
Friouwulf (peace-wolf)
Hengest (avenger-ruler)
Wigfrip (war-peace)
Wulfgifu (wolf-gift)
Wulfstan (wolf-stone)
Wulfwig (wolf-war)

SCANDINAVIAN TRAIL of WORDS

Viking sea raiders from Denmark, Sweden, and Norway sought nearby treasure which lured them to ravage the coastline settlements of Scotland and England about 750 B.C. Some raiders settled permanently.

4

The Scandinavians had no surnames. Examples of names in 800 A.D. include:

Osborne (Asbiorn, "god-bear")
Booth (Bothe, "herdsman")
Secker (Sekkr, "sackmaker")
Woolf (Uhlfr, "wolf-cunning")
Seagram (Saegrmr, "sea-guardian")
Knowles (Knol, "turnip-headed")
Knott (Knutr, "square-bodied")
Osmond (Asmindr, "the protector")

Danish, Swedish, and Norwegian words of today:

ask (ash)
blad (leaf or blade)
blom (bloom)
dotter (daughter)
ey (island)
fisk (fish)

gron (green)
havn (haven)
kaka (cake)
nas (nose)
ost (east)
strom (stream)

FRENCH TRAIL of WORDS

The Norman-French conquerors (1066 A.D.) established a new language trail in Angleland, where Anglo-Saxons reluctantly tried to learn French. By 1200 A.D. the Anglo-Saxons shunned use of the French language, finding the nasal pitch and shrill blends an impossible challenge for their guttural-toned Germanic speech patterns. To avoid using the conquerors' language, they interwove Anglo-Saxon words into the French sentences, creating an Anglo-Norman pattern of daily common speech.

Below is a list of American names and their Norman-French roots from the Middle Ages. The spelling and pronunciation of the French names indicate the changes in our surnames through nine hundred years of name-history. The American names below can be found in most U.S.A. telephone books.

5

NORMAN-FR. ROOTS	U.S.A. SURNAMES
Alisaundre*	Saunders
Baron	Baron
Beauchamp	Beecham
Beuzeville	Boswell
Blancart	Blanchard
Boulogne	Boleyn
Candelier	Chandler
Caplain	Chaplain
d'Aubigny	Dabney
d'Isigny	Disney
du L'Eau	Waters
Fauconnier	Faulkner
fil de Simon	FitzSimmons
Gaiolere	Gaylor
Geuffroi	Jeffrey
Guillot	Gillette
Fourdon	Gordon
deGuillaume	Williams
Hernais	Ernest
Herriot	Harris
Jourdain	Jordan
Maillet	Mallet
Maloret	Mallory
Magneville	Mandeville
Nourice	Norris
Per Dieu	Purdue-Pardee
Portier	Porter
Rivoire	Revere
St. Aubin	Tobin
St. Clair	Sinclair
St. Denis	Sidney
St. Mark	Seamark
St. Maur	Seymour
St. Paul	Semple
St. Pierre	Semper
Tailleur	Taylor

*The Norman-French brought the name of Alisaundre to England in 1066 A.D. and it became a very popular first name in Scotland as *Alexander*. Nicknames springing from *Alexander* include: Alec, Alex, Alister, Alistair, Ellick, Sander, Sanders, Sandy, and Saunders.

FRENCH and ANGLO-SAXON TRAILS of WORDS

-- A tall and gaunt, blue-eyed storyteller in the court of King Henry VIII began a Chaucerian tale:

A knight there was, and that a worthy man,
That fro the time that he first bigan
To riden, he loved chivalrye,
Trouthe and honour, freedom, and courteisye.
Ful worthy was he in his lordes werre,
And thereto hadde he riden (no man ferre),
As wel in Christendom as hethenesse. --

The Anglo-Saxons envied the French-Normans' "finer things of life," and easily accepted French words such as: gown, satin, robe, dress, fashion, ruby, pearl, sapphire, and diamond. The superiority of French cooking added: sauce, boil, fry, stew, roast, and pie to the Anglo-Saxons' vocabulary. In turn, the French used Anglo-Saxon words for: baker, potter, brewer, smith, cook, and herder to identify "common" servants.

The English Royal court in 1300 A.D. issued edicts that included French and Anglo-Saxon words. In 1380 A.D. this new Anglish (English) became the official language for Oxford and Cambridge universities. By 1400 A.D. Chaucer's Canterbury Tales established the narrowing difference between fourteenth century Anglish (English) and today's English usage.

7

Shakespeare's death in 1616 A.D. came at a time of fervent English nationalism: language and literature now were one hundred percent English. French words were considered to be a foreign import, occasionally spoken at the British royal court by religious notables and aristocratic visitors from France.

ENGLISH TRAIL of WORDS

-- A tall and gaunt, blue-eyed man leaped ashore. He strode into a wilderness of winter, his old-world boots crunching a new trail in freshly-fallen snow. Ahead were days and days of miles and miles before he would catch up with the spring season of a ready-made English-speaking nation in the unspoiled New World. --

Below is the Pilgrim passenger list of the *Mayflower* when it landed at Plymouth Rock cove in Massachusetts on 21 November 1620:

PASSENGER	MEANING	TYPE
ALDEN	old friend	Nickname
BILLINGSTON	lived in Billington	Address
BRADFORD	resided by wide stream	Address
BREWSTER	female ale brewer	Occupation
BRITTERIDGE	lived near steep ridge	Address
BROWN	of dark skin or hair	Nickname
CARTER	drove small cart/wagon	Occupation
CARVER	a woodcarver	Occupation
CHELTON	lived in Chilton village	Address
CLARKE	the man of learning	Occupation
COOKE	a food preparer	Occupation
CRACKSTON	lived in Crackston village	Address
DOTEY	the strong, brave man	Nickname
EATON	lived in Eaton village	Address
ELLIS	son or descendant of Ellis	Parent
ENGLISH	born in England	Address
FLETCHER	maker & seller of arrows	Occupation

8

FULLER	a washer of new cloth	Occupation
GARDINER	tended a large garden	Occupation
GOODMAN	the good, likeable man	Nickname
HOLEBECK	lived in Holebeck village	Address
HOPKINS	son of Hob or Robert	Parent
HOWLAND	lived on a hill	Address
LANGEMORE	lived on a long moor	Address
LEISTER	lived in Leicester village	Address
MARGESON	son of Marge or Margaret	Parent
MARTIN	son of Martin	Parent
MOORE	dark-skinned, like a Moor	Nickname
MULLINS	lived near a grain mill	Address
PRIEST	a minister	Occupation
RIDGATE	lived near a ridge	Address
ROGERS	son of Roger	Parent
SAMSON	son of Samuel	Parent
SOULE	lived near a muddy pond	Address
STANDISH	lived at a stony place	Address
STORY	the strong, powerful man	Nickname
THOMPSON	son of Thomas	Parent
TILLEY	son/descendant of Matilda	Parent
TINKER	mends pots/pans/kettles	Occupation
TREVORE	lived in Trevore	Address
TURNER	made objects on a lathe	Occupation
WARNER	a forest game warden	Occupation
WHITE	of light hair or skin	Nickname
WILDER	lived in a forest	Address
WINSLOW	lived in Winslow	Address

Family names are always around us: in our daily conversation, in newspapers, or on radio and television programs. Many persons take great pride in their names and are concerned that their surname pass into the future without any changes.

We have honored famous family names from American history by using them to identify cities, schools, colleges, libraries, fire stations, steamships, and more.

It is a pleasant surprise to learn that one's own family name is a constant reminder of an ancestor's daily "needs and deeds" and "ways and days" of life

9

in a castle, village, or church during the Middle Ages.

- QUESTIONS...QUESTIONS -

Name historians have these questions in mind when they try to trace an ancestor's name:

When was the name first used to identify the ancestor?
Was the name Latin, Anglo-Saxon, French, Celtic, or Scandinavian?
What was the name's meaning?
What were its changes in use or spelling by 1900 A.D.?
What is today's spelling of this name?

For example, eight hundred years of *Stanley*:

1100 A.D. - *Stanley* was a Middle Ages identification for the ancestor who lived in or near a stony field. Its Old English root was *stan* (stone) and *leah* (field or meadow), identifying the ancestor "who lived in a stony, open space". It was spelled *Stanlai* and *Stanlay* by the year 1150. It was not used as a first name in the Middle Ages.

1250-1500 A.D. - When a small village developed at this cleared open space, it was place-named *Stanlai* in remembrance of its first resident. Later, some of its residents took *Stanley* as a family name.

1875-1910 A.D. - Sir Henry Morton Stanley, a famous explorer of far-away Africa, became popular in England by 1875. His earliest ancestor probably once resided in *Stanley* village. By 1885, the explorer's family name had become a favorite first name for boys in England, Scotland, Wales, Australia, Canada, and America.

1925-1980 A.D. - By 1925, *Stanley* as a first name was no longer popular in America, yet as a surname *Stanley* has had considerable listings in our phone-

books.   Name-historian Elsdon C. Smith has estimated that there are more than 85,000 Americans
with the family name of *Stanley*.

- - - - - - - - - -

Hero-worship in the nineteenth century
influenced Americans to use famous
family names as first names for boys:
Washington, Jefferson, Lincoln, Lee,
and Jackson.   Religious parents often
selected such names as: Luther, Wes-
ley,   and   Calvin   for   their   sons.
Homer, Virgil, Byron, and Milton, the
names of famous authors, were also
popular choices for boys' names in the
nineteenth century.

- - - - - - - - - -

- OF NAMES WE NEVER CHOSE -

Name-historians are able to trace many phonebook
names all the way back to the conquering of England by
the Norman-French in 1066 A.D.   To a name-historian
such family names are a special kind of language and
history fossil because many of our American family
names have lost the meanings they had when these same
names once identified a long-ago ancestor.   For
example:

Armstrong originally identified the person who had
great strength of body.   Many of the thousands of
Armstrongs listed in today's phonebooks do <u>not</u> have
unusally strong arms.

Ballard originally identifed the person who was bald-
headed.   Many of the thousands of *Ballards* in our
phonebooks are <u>not</u> bald-headed.

Crockett originally identified the person who was
crippled.   Many of the thousands of *Crocketts* in today's
phonebooks are <u>not</u> crippled.

11

Spencer originally identifed the person who was in charge of food supplies in a castle. Not many *Spencers* today dispense food for a living.

O'Neill originally identified the Irish person who was an athlete of great fame. Most of the *O'Neills* in today's phonebooks are <u>not</u> famous athletes.

Tuttle (*Tuthill*) originally identified the person who tooted a horn from his post within a castle tower to warn of approaching horsemen. *Tuttles* listed in today's phonebooks are <u>not</u> employed as castle lookouts!

Marshall originally identified the person who was in charge of horses. Most of today's *Marshalls* are <u>not</u> expert horse doctors or trainers.

CHAPTER 2

HOW OUR FAMILY NAMES BEGAN

At the beginning of the Middle Ages (1050-1500 A.D.) our ancestors in England, Ireland, Scotland, and Wales used only a first name to identify themselves. The most popular male names were William, Robert, Richard, Walter, and Ralph. The most popular names for girls were Anne, Matilda, Agnes, Margery, and Isobel.

Our ancestors used four ways to identify a person by the use of a description which eventually became a second or family name: NICKNAME, OCCUPATION or TRADE, FIRST NAME of a parent, and ADDRESS or LOCATION.

NICKNAME:

>> Katherine *Doolittle* (the lazy one)
>> Walter *Ballard* (the bald-headed one)
>> Anne *White* (the blond-haired one)
>> Edgar *Bunche* (the hunch-backed one)

OCCUPATION or TRADE:

>> Agnes *Webster* (a female weaver)
>> Roland *Coward* (a cow herder)
>> Brian *Bowles* (a maker of wooden bowls)

> Alice who-worked-as-a-baker became today's
>> Alice *Baker* or *Baxter*.

13

FIRST NAME of parent:

> Harold *Johnson* (son of John)
> Henry *Annison* (son of Annie)
> Albert *Wilson* (the son of Will or William)
> Roger *Margeson* (son of Marge)

ADDRESS or LOCATION:

> Edward *Gates* (lived near the castle gates)
> Margaret *Cauldwell* (lived near the cold well)
> Ann *Swindell* (lived near the valley pig farm)
> Alfred *Atwood* (lived in the woods)

> > Alice who-lived-(or-worked)-in-the-cottage-at-the-north-corner-of-the-village became today's Alice *Northcott* or *Norcutt*.

> > William who-lived-(or-worked)-near-the-church-on-the-hill became today's William *Churchill*.

The ancestor who lived in the end cottage became known as *Endicott*; at the edge of town, *Townsend*; in a pear grove, *Perriman*; at a large hall, *Halstead*; near a cheese wick, *Chessick*; by a roadside cross, *Crosby*; near the priest's cottage *Prescott*; by a castle laundry shed, *Landry*; near holly trees, *Hollins*; on an island of many birds, *Birdseye*.

From 1100 A.D. to 1300 A.D. these second names frequently changed:

Perhaps William *Churchill* no longer lived near the church on the hill. He now worked as the toll-collector on the village bridge. People soon referred to him as William the *Tollman*.

Perhaps Agnes *Northcott* moved to another village where she worked as a weaver of cloth. Now she was identified as Agnes the *Webster* (the female version of *Weaver*).

By 1150 A.D. it became the custom and fashion for the lords of castles or plantations (manors) to take a second name of identity. Such a name usually was the identity of the castle or manor that a nobleman owned:

Robert - Lord of *Greystone* Castle
Leslie - Earl of *Oakfield* Hall
Wallace - Duke of *Norwich* Manor

The names of these estates were passed on from eldest child to the eldest child.

By 1250 A.D. these estate names had become inherited family names and were used even when a son or daughter moved away from the estate.

Gradually, through the later years of the Middle Ages, the lower classes of persons in England imitated the "family name" custom of the nobility and by 1500 A.D. almost everybody's last name had become an inherited surname.

- An ANCESTOR's HOLIDAY
on a PLANTATION in the MIDDLE AGES -

September 29, 1261 A.D. was the holy day of Michael mas. It was a holiday on the plantation of the Duke of Ridgeton, fifty miles north from the Thames River in England. No one had to work on such a holy day. Also it was the day for farm tenants to pay their *tallage* (rent) for the use of the nobleman's land.

Thirty-two men and eleven women sat or stood in the large grassy yard behind the Duke's large barn. Shouts of children at play on the nearby village green could be heard.

Finally the Duke and his clerk (*Clark*) arrived on horseback. The crowd of tenants suddenly silenced, rose to their feet and bowed their heads. The clerk clapped his hands and asked the tenants to form a single line. One by one each tenant approached the clerk who had a large leather pouch in which he put the rent payments he was collecting. Every rent payment was recorded in a book the clerk had brought.

After the collection of *tallages* the clerk asked, "Who has *heriot* (death fine) and *mortuary* (cemetery expense) to pay?" Widow Kate-atte-pear-tree (Kate *Perry*) came forward to report her husband had died two days ago. She offered the Duke the *heriot* of a pig because the nobleman had lost a worker. She also offered a *mortuary* of thirty eggs for permission to bury her husband in the local church cemetery. The Duke raised his gloved right hand to the clerk, signaling the Duke's acceptance of the widow's gifts.

Richard-the-priest's servantman (Richard *Pressman*) asked for a *merchet* (permission for his daughter to be married). The Duke agreed and accepted five geese as a gift from Richard.

Then the clerk asked, "Who wishes to have *wood penny* (permission to collect dead wood in the Duke's forest)?" The following tenants came forward to pay the clerk a penny for this wood-gathering privilege:

ANCESTOR'S NAME	TODAY'S NAME
Griff-the-cow-herder	Griffith COWARD
Robin-the-chartier	Robin CARTER
Widow Ann-at-the-cold-well	Ann CAULDWELL
Geoff-who-could-turn-a-bull	Jeff TURNBULL
Wat-atte-the-oaks	Walter OAKLAND
Roger-the-goode-one	Roger GOODMAN
Piers-with-small-head	Peter SMOLLETT
William-the-goat-herder	William GOTHARD
Tom-the-cheese-maker	Tom CHESSMAN
Martin-atte-the-sheep-stalk	Martin SHEPLEY
Alfred-the-yeats-keeper	Alfred GATES
Matilda-atte-the-pear-tree	Matilda PERRY

16

Hugh-atte-the-wet-land	Hugh WHITAKER
Albert-the-wool-packer	Albert PACKARD
Bettie-atte-deer-meadow	Bettie RALEIGH

Ben-le-bald-head (Ben *Ballard*) came forward to ask the Duke for a *relief* (privilege): Ben wished to farm his father's strip of land, for the old man had become too feeble to work. The Duke granted this request, asking three shillings of *tallage* (rent payment). Ben knelt before the nobleman, touched his forehead to the ground, loudly thanking the nobleman for his kindness and generosity.

Dick-the-newcomer (Dick *Newman*) requested *mill penny* (permission to grind his grain at the Duke's mill). The clerk granted permission and accepted a coin from Dick.

The last person to make a request was Roger-the-swine-herder (Roger *Swinnard*). He wanted permission for his son Allyn to join a nearby monastery where Allyn could enroll to become a monk. The Duke warmly praised Allyn for his desire to serve God in this special way.

The nobleman then gave Allyn permission to join the nearby monastery with this condition: Allyn must give the Duke ten *boon-days* (ten days of free labor at haymaking and harvesting times) for three years. Allyn dropped on his knees to graciously thank the nobleman, promising always to be available for service to the Duke.

The Duke waved his hand in farewell to the tenants as he and his clerk rode away toward the large estate-house. The crowd of tenants quickly dispersed to the grassy churchyard to watch a special Michaelmas pageant which featured a short play about Saint Michael.

A roast goose supper in the churchyard concluded this holy day in honor of archangel Michael.

CHAPTER 3

10% of our FAMILY NAMES
come from NICKNAMES

The Old English (O.E.) root for nickname was *ekename*, meaning "the also or added name".

Youngsters quickly get to know who everyone else is in a small school. They make jokes or exchange opinions about one another, often inventing nicknames for fellow students. The fat boy or girl becomes Tubby, Fatso, or Tiny. The slender one may be called Skinny or Spider. Rusty is a frequent name for a red-headed boy, and High Pockets for a long-legged girl.

People who lived in a small village in the Middle Ages knew everyone in their settlement. They, too, joked and gossiped about each other. Nicknames were easy to invent, for everyone knew a great deal about each other's personality and physical characteristics. A person with a large head might be called Broadhead or Bullitt (bullish). A thin person was nicknamed Baines (bones) or Spriggs (sprig of a bush). The very tall one was identified as Longfellow, Crane, or Biggs.

Below is a list of some nicknames discovered in various church and tax records in medieval England. Notice that these nicknames offer English language clues to pronounciation and spelling during the thirteenth, fourteenth, and fifteenth centuries:

19

Thirteenth century:

Blakbeird
Likfinger
Priggmouth
Pudding

Fourteenth century:

Buttermouth
Cokeye
Dogetail
Domesoft
Prettyman
Rotenhering
Swetemouth

Fifteenth century:

Catskin
Harepyn
Shepewassh

- SOME KIND AND UNKIND NICKNAMES IN OUR PHONEBOOKS -

Abbot was a teasing nickname for the ancestor who walked about in a manner of "be as holy a person as I am". *Abbot* later became a respectable family name and appears frequently in today's phone books.

Ambler was a teasing kind of nickname for the ancestor who walked or "ambled" like a slow-moving horse in a plowed field.

April identified the person with behavior as unpredictable as that month's weather; the name arose from our ancestors living during the Middle Ages who were keenly observant of the changes of seasons. Through several centuries the nickname *April* changed to *Averill*.

Averill is an infrequent name in today's phonebooks. *Averill* occasionally has been given as a first name in America. See *April*.

Ayers identified the ancestor who was the heir (or son of the heir) to an estate. Root: O.E. *eir*.

Bellamy is a pleasant-sounding name rooted in the Norman-French *bel* (beautiful) and *ami* (friend).

Bishop was a teasing nickname for the ancestor who walked about in a manner of "be as holy a person as I am". *Bishop* later became a respectable family name and is quite numerous in today's phone books.

Bliss identified a happy and likable person. Root: O.E. *blis*.

Blythe identified a happy and likable person. Root: O.E. *blithe*.

Bonner is a frequent phone book listing. It arises from the Norman-French *boners* (the good guy), identifying the gentle and polite ancestor.

Brisbane was the name for the prison torturer who broke the arms and legs of a dangerous prisoner to prevent the latter's escape. *Brisbane* is rooted in the Norman-French *bris* (break) and the Scottish *ban* (bone).

From the Norman-French *bon-coeur* (good-hearted person) came today's nickname of *Bunker*.

Burnand was a nickname for the dungeon torturer who branded a thief's hands.

- - - - - - - - -

Why do we say CAUGHT RED-HANDED? A person was guilty of a crime during the Middle Ages only if he or she confessed it or was caught

21

committing the crime. To butcher someone else's cow, pig, or sheep was a very common yet serious crime in those days. Possession of such fresh meat was not proof of this felony. The thief had to be caught with the slaughtered animal's blood on his hands. Thus to catch a thief by surprise gave us today's expression: CAUGHT RED-HANDED.

- - - - - - - - - -

Caudel was a warm liquid, mixed with wine or ale, spices, and grain. It was served to sick persons. A medieval ancestor who easily sickened from an alcoholic drink was perhaps teased with the suggestion, "You'd best sip only caudel!" Hence his nickname of *Caudell*. Root: Norman-French *caudel* (porridge or broth).

Chiles is a frequent variation of *Childe* used in southeastern America. See *Childe*.

Childe. By the fourteenth century, many English towns had an orphanage which was usually called "Childers House." Today's phone book listings of *Childe*, *Childers*, and *Childs* were nicknames long ago for orphaned ancestors.

Childers see *Childe*.

Childs see *Childe*.

Cock. Lively and cheerful medieval servant lads and lassies who were inclined to be "saucy or "cocky" usually were the butt of that kind of nickname – Adam (*Adcock*); Anne (*Ancock*); Barbara (*Babcock*); John or Joan (*Joncock*); Henry (*Hancock*); and Will (*Wilcock*). By the seventeenth century English dialectal differences shifted *Babcock* into *Babcox*, *Wilcock* into *Wilcox*, etc. Root: O.E. *cocc* (as cocky as a rooster).

22

The ancestor who tended fires on a battlefield or in a castle usually slept near such a fireplace or bonfire. He earned the label of *Coleman*, from the root of the Old English *col-mann* (coalman).

Cooney was an Irish nickname for an "elegant" ancestor. Root: Irish *cuanam* (refined one).

Coote and *Couts* were name-labels for a person "stupid as a coot bird". Root: O.E. *cot* (coot).

Couts see *Coote*.

The young ancestor who was as romantic as a dove was nicknamed *Culver*. Root: O.E. *culfre* (dove or pigeon).

Curtis is from the Norman-French *curteis* (courteous). *Curtis* is sometimes spelled, *Curtoys*.

Curtoys see *Curtis*.

David was pronounced *Daffid* in Wales in the Middle Ages. "Taffie" was a Welsh nickname for *David*. "Taffie" is used today in America as a female first name.

Dillard see *Dolling*.

Dollard see *Dolling*.

Dolling. A dull or slow-witted person was frequently nicknamed *Dolling* in Anglo-Saxon times (eleventh century). In medieval England this became *Dowling*, *Dillard*, and *Dollard*.

The lazy, good-for-nothing ancestor was called *Doolittle*.

Doran was an Irish nickname for a stranger or newly arrived person.

Dowling see *Dolling*.

23

If an ancestor was too poor to buy ale, he was often nicknamed *Drinkwater*.

Eames was a complimentary nickname for the son of an uncle.

An eagle-eyed ancestor probably enjoyed his complimentary nickname of *Eagle*. Root: O. Fr. *aigle* (eagle).

The eagle also gave us today's phone book name of *Early*. Root: A.S. *earlic* (eagle).

Egan was a frequent Irish nickname for a very active and full-of-life ancestor. Root: Gaelic *aodhagan*.

English was a frequent nickname in Scotland, Ireland, and Wales for an ancestor who came from England. Root: O.E. *englisc*.

Ennion or *Eynon* was a Welsh ancestral nickname, from the Welsh *eninon* (anvil), identifying the person who was as sturdy and longlasting as an anvil.

Eynon see *Ennion*.

From the Irish *ionnrachtaigh* (the criminal) came today's name of *Enright*.

Ennis identified the ancestor who was "very unusual". Root: Irish *aonghuis*.

Fagan was an uncomplimentary nickname for the awkward, clumsy person.

Fitch is a frequent listing in our phone books. It was an uncomplimentary medieval nickname, identifying the ancestor who was "as wicked as a weasel". Root: O.E. *fitche* (weasel or polecat).

War, disease, and famine were responsible for the very high percentage of medieval orphans. An ancestor who lived in a foster home was frequently named *Foster*. Root: O.E. *fostre*.

The clever and cunning ancestor who was always regarded with suspicion usually was nicknamed *Fox*. Root: O.E. *fox*. *Foxx* is a modern spelling.

The ancestor born in the cold, frosty winter season often was named *Frost*. Root: O.E. *frost*.

Galbraith nicknamed an overseas immigrant or stranger in Scotland. Root: Gaelic *gall* (stranger) and *Bhreathnach* (Briton).

Galloway nicknamed an overseas immigrant or stranger in Scotland. Root: Gaelic *gallgaidhe* (the stranger or foreigner).

Galt nicknamed an overseas immigrant or stranger in Scotland. Root: Gaelic *gall* (stranger).

Gault was an English medieval nickname for a stranger or newly arrived person.

Gaylord was a complimentary nickname for a happy-go-lucky person.

The Welsh nickname for the ancestor with very odd behavior was *Gerrish* (the madman). Root: Welsh *gervshe*.

Gill was an Irish nickname for a stranger or newly arrived person.

Good must have been a favorite yet overused English medieval word. It was combined with other words to give us complimentary nicknames for some of our ancestors: *Goodbody, Goodchild, Goodenough, Good-fellow, Goodfriend, Goodhart, Goodjohn, Goodkin, Goodrich,* and *Goodson.* *Good* and *Goode* are frequent phone book listings.

Goodhue long ago was *Goodhugh*, identifying "the good servant". *Goodhue* also was a nickname for an ancestor who was "a good guy".

Goodman, from the Anglo-Saxon *godmund*, is a frequent phone book listing.

The not-too-frequent *Goodspeed* was a nickname that poked fun at the ancestor who overused, "God speed you!"

From the Old English *god* (good) and *wine* (friend) came today's phone book listing of *Goodwin*.

Goodyear was a teasing kind of nickname for an ancestor who always greeted a person with the question, "What the good year?" (How are things with you?).

Guest was a complimentary nickname for the welcome stranger.

Gulliver was an uncomplimentary nickname for a greedy eater.

Haggard was a medieval descriptive word for a trained hawk that became a wild bird again. It was also for a youth "who behaved like a hagard" (wild hawk). Root: O. Fr. *hagard* (unta med wild).

Haldane dates back to medieval Danish colonization in England. *Haldane* is rooted in Old Danish *healf* (half) and *dan* (Dane), identifying the ancestor with one Danish parent.

Haliliday see *Holliday*.

Hardy was a worthy nickname for the ancestor who was of daring and bold character.

The Norman-French introduced the name of *Hillary* into Britain. St. Hilarius was an early French priest of great popularity, beloved for his great sense of humor and merry personality. Root: Norman-French *hilaire* (the hilarious one). HILLARY is listed in many of today's phone books. It sometimes is used today as a female first name.

Hogg was a medieval nickname for an ancestor "bold and fearless as a boar (hog)", the most ferocious of all British wild animals. Root: O.E. *hogg*.

Holliday. Middle Ages ancestors believed that it was a special blessing from God for a baby to be born on a holiday (*haeligdaeg* or holy day), bequeathing to us the nicknames of *Haliliday* and *Holliday*.

- - - - - - - - - -

There were at least sixty meatless holy days in the Middle Ages. On such holidays our English ancestors usually ate a type of flat fish (flounder) they called "holy butt". Today we say it as "halibut".

- - - - - - - - - -

Inglis see *Inglish*.

Inglish. During the early Middle Ages the lord of a

plantation rarely permitted his serfs to leave the village. Occasionally a serf managed to buy his freedom giving him the right to live and work wherever he pleased. When an English ancestral "freeman" migrated into Wales, Ireland, or Scotland, he usually was nicknamed *Inglish*, *Inglis*, or *Ingliss*. Because his pronunciation and accent were different, he was identified as "the stranger among us".

Innes (*Innis*) is an Irish nickname from *aonghuis* (the best one).

Innis see *Innes*.

Ireland and *Irish* were emigrant nicknames used mainly by the English. These two names usually are of equal frequency in U.S.A. phone books.

Irish see *Ireland*.

Jarmain. A German immigrant in medieval Britain was referred to as "the German," but it was often also spelled as *Jarmain* or *Jarman*.

Jarman see *Jarmain*.

The ancestor who jabbered non-stop received the nickname of *Jay* (chattering jay bird) for the rest of the chatterer's life.

Jewett identified the "little Jew".

Kaiser is German for *King*.

Keen was a complimentary nickname for the wise, reasonable person.

Kellogg is a famous American name for the manufacturer of corn flakes and other breakfast foods. In the Middle Ages it was a nickname for the butcher who specialized in killing hogs (kill hog); it was spelled *Kelehoge* in the fourteenth century.

The Irish ancestor "always ready to argue or fight" was labeled *Kelly*. Root: Gaelic *ceallaigh*.

An ancestor who acted the role of a king in a religious festival year after year was usually nicknamed *King*. Root: O.E. *cyng* (king).

Kiser is the English version of the German *Kaiser* (king).

Kyser is the English version of the German *Kaiser*.

Lamb(e), *Lambie*, *Lambey*, *Lambkin*, *Lamden*, and *Lumpkin* were instant nicknames for the meek, lamblike fellow (Scottish or English).

Norman-Frenchmen in England in the eleventh and twelfth centuries said "L'Anglois" when they referred to an Englishman. By the fourteenth century Englishmen said *Langley* instead of "L'Anglois.".

Lark was a complimentary nickname for an ancestor who was a pleasing singer. Root: O.E. *lawerce* (lark).

Lem(m)on was the admired lover or sweetheart. Root: O.E. *leman* (loved one).

Linnet(te) often identified the ancestor who was "as noisy and nervous" as a linnet bird. Root: O.E. *linete*.

Lovejoy identified the ancestor who "loved the best pleasures of life".

Lovelace nicknamed the English ancestor who was "unloved". It also was used to tease the Scottish fellow who "greatly loved the lassies".

From Norman-French *maleure* (bad luck) came the uncomplimentary nickname of *Mallory* for an unlucky person.

Meek(s) identified the shy, timid ancestor.

Meredith meant "the man of excellence".   Root: Welsh *mawreddog*.

Merriam was a complimentary nickname for someone who was always cheerful.

Merriman see *Merrlam*.

Merriweather see *Merrlam*.

Merrlam.   The cheerful, happy-go-lucky ancestor was variously named *Merrlam*, *Merriman* (from Robin Hood's time), or *Merriweather*.

Monday or *Mundy* identified the infant who was abandoned at a church or orphanage on a Monday.

As a nickname, *Moody* suggests a tempermental ancestor, yet it actually meant "bold and brave soldier".

Mooney was an Irish medieval nickname for a wealthy ancestor.   Root: Gaelic *maonaigh* (money).

Morgan was a Welsh nickname for the person born in a seaside place.   Root: Welsh *mor* (sea) and *gan* (birth).

Mundy see *Monday*.

Murphy was an Irish nickname for a sea-fighting man.   Root: Gaelic *murchada*.

Neave or *Nieve(s)* identified the nephew ancestor. It also ridiculed the fellow who was a spendthrift or "good-for-nothing".

Neil(1) is a many-listed Irish nickname in today's phone book and it has even more listings in the O'Neill columns.   Root: Irish *niall* (the champion). *Neill* was always popular in Ireland (most often as

MacNeill or *O'Neill*). Through nine hundred years
of name history, the nickname of *Neil(1)* has spread
at least fifteen variations through Scotland, Wales,
and England:

Nahill - Ir.	*Neylan* - Welsh
Neal(e) - Eng.	*Niall* - Welsh
Neild - Ir.	*Niel* - Scot.
Neils - Ir.	*Nigel* - Scot.
Neilson - Eng.	*Nihall* - Eng.
Nelligan - Ir.	*Nihill* - Eng.
Nellis - Ir.	*Niland* - Ir.
Nelson - Eng.	

Newcomb was an English nickname for a stranger
or newly arrived person.

A newly arrived person (*Newman*) in a medieval village usually was regarded with fear or suspicion.
Sometimes he lived in the village for several years
before he became accepted by the other residents as
an equal. *Newman* is a many-listed nickname in
American phone books.

Nieve(s) see *Neave*.

Niven or *Nivin(s)* was a complimentary Irish nickname for the ancestor whose life-style was
saintlike. Root: Irish *naomhin* (the saint).

Noah. The ancestor who acted the part of Noah in
a "Noah's Ark" church pageant usually was nicknamed *Noah*. *Noe* is a later English variation.

Noel. It was a Norman-French custom to name a
baby *Noel* when he or she was born on Christmas
day. *Nowell* was a later variation. Root: Norman-
French *noel* (Christmas).

Norman was a nickname for a Frenchman from
Normandy. It also identified the immigrant ancestor
from Norway (the man from the north).

31

Nowell see *Noel.*

- - - - - - - - - -

Seventh century Anglo-Saxon Princess Audrey founded a nunnery in 672 A.D. Legend has it that she died of a throat ailment caused by her sinful habit of wearing brilliant colored neck scarves. She was sainted soon after her early death, and the annual St. Audrey's Fair commemorates her birthday. Nuns from her convent sold strips of "St. Audrey's lace" to be worn at the throat; these strips of lace were of good quality. Over the years the quality of the lace strips became inferior. Medieval common speech corrupted "St. Audrey's lace" into "Tawdry's lace". By 1500 A.D., in England, "tawdy" identified any kind of shoddy merchandise.

- - - - - - - - - -

Nunn(e) is a listing in many phone books, identifying the ancestor who was "as timid and shy as a nun". *Nunn(e)* also was a nickname for a descendant of a nun. Root: O.E. *nunne.*

- - - - - - - - - -

Why do we say it? Your dictionary defines bedlam as a "scene of noise and confusion."

The Hospital of St. Mary of Bethlehem was founded in 1257 A.D. as a place of temporary residence for visiting church notables and religious leaders. By the end of the fifteenth century the hospital functioned as an asylum for the insane. For a small

32

fee, Londoners were permitted to enter and view these insane patients in their barred cells.

Folk speech soon corrupted "Bethlehem" into "bedlam". Eventually "bedlam" generally described any scene of confusion, turmoil, or uproar. A homeless lunatic in an English village often was taunted as "Tom o'Bedlam" or "Bess o'Bedlam".

– – – – – – – – – –

Pace see *Peace.*

Paine and *Payne* are from the Old French *paien* (pagan), identifying the crude countryside peasant or an unbaptized ancestor.

Most medieval persons rarely left their villages. Among those few who did were a handful of holy persons who made a religious pilgrimage to France or Italy. A few of these were able to make the dangerous trip to the Holy Land on the Mediterranean Sea. For the return journey such a pilgrim carried a palm branch as a sign he had completed a special pilgrimage, earning him the honored nickname of *Palmer*, a much-listed name in our phone books today.

Pardee was an English nickname for the ancestor who overused the Norman-French oath "Per Dieu! Per Dieu!" (By God! By God!). *Pardew*, *Perdue*, *Perdy*, *Purdy*, and *Purdue* were later English variations for *Pardee*.

Parson, *Pope*, and *Priest* were teasing nicknames for an ancestor who walked about in a manner of "be as holy a person as I am". These nicknames later became respectable family names and all are quite numerous in today's phone books.

Payne see *Paine*.

Peace was a nickname often used for a child born at Easter time. Root: Norman-French *pais* (peace). *Pace* was its frequent medieval spelling.

Perdue see *Pardee*.

Perdy see *Pardee*.

The medieval ancestor from Portugal was called *Pettingill* (the Anglo-Saxon pronunciation for Portugal).

Pidgeon see *Pigeon*.

Pigeon identified the ancestor considered to be easily deceived or swindled. Root: Norman-French *pipjon*, sometimes spelled *pidgen* or *pidgon* in the Middle Ages. The pigeon also was a medieval love symbol because of its billing and cooing sounds, and was a handy name tag for a newlywed or a lovesick ancestor.

Pope see *Parson*.

Powers is from the Old French *povere* (the poor one). It is a many-listed nickname in today's phone books.

Pratt was an uncomplimentary nickname for a tricky, sly person.

Priest see *Parson*.

Pride or *Pryde* identified the medieval actor who played the part of Pride in a religious pageant.

Prince, from the Norman-French *prince*, nicknamed medieval actors in a religious festival.

Prophet, from the Norman-French *prophete*, nicknamed medieval actors in a religious festival.

Pryde see *Pride*.

Purdue see *Pardee*.

Purdy see *Pardee*.

A quail bird was considered to be a simple, timid creature; and *Quayle* became a frequent nickname for the ancestor with a similar temperament. Root: Norman-French *quaille*.

An Anglo-Saxon ancestor whose battle shield had a wolf's head painted on it gave us today's *Randall*, a many-listed nickname in our phone books. Root: Anglo-Saxon *rand-wulf* (wolf's head).

Reagan see *Regan*.

Reese was a Welsh nickname for the ancestor full of affection. Root O. Wel *ris* (the loving person).

Re(a)gan is a Irish nickname for "the little chieftan". Root: Irish *reagain*.

Rex and *Roy* are English variations for *King*.

Sayce was a Welsh nickname for a stranger or newly arrived person.

Sealey or *Seeley* were nicknames of approval for the happy-go-lucky ancestor. Root: O.E. *saelig* (full of goodness).

Sharp(e) is a much-listed phone book family name which began as a nickname for a person of high intelligence. Root: O.E. *scarp* (sharp).

Smart was a nickname for a keen-minded person.

Snelling was a nickname for a keen-minded person.

A child born in a heavy *Snow* storm often went through life with such a birth event as a nickname.

Sparkes was a nickname for a keen-minded person.

Sprague was a nickname for a keen-minded and lively person.

Springer was a complimentary nickname for the can't-sit-still person.

Suspicion and mistrust of a foreigner in a Middle Ages village gave us the nickname of *Strange*, a frequent telephone book listing. Root: O. Fr. *estrange* (stranger).

A child born on *Sunday* went through life with such a birth event as a nickname.

Taber and *Tabor* identified the ancestor who played a drum. Root: O. Fr. *tabour*.

Talmadge was a nickname for a villager always seen with a knapsack on his back. Root: O. Fr. *telemache* (knapsack).

The ancestor who, as an infant, was abandoned in a temple, was sometimes nicknamed *Temple* (a frequent phone book listing). Root: O.E. *tempel*.

Tiffany was a medieval name for girls born on the holy day of Epiphany. It survived through the centuries as a family name. Root: Latin *theophains* and O. Fr. *tipbaine*.

Todd is a family name of many phone book listings, identifying a cunning and scheming ancestor. Root: O.E. *todde* (the foxy one).

The ancestor who was a high-stepping dancer of skill usually was nicknamed *Tripp* or *Tripper*. Root: O.E. *trippere* (dancer).

Truman nicknamed a faithful and loyal ancestor.

The Irish nickname for "the glorious warrior" was *Tunney*, from the Irish *tonnaigh*.

A sinful ancestor often was nicknamed *Turpin*. Root: O. Fr. *tourpin* (the immoral one).

Today's phone book family name of *Veasey* was also spelled as *Vaisey*, *Vezey*, and *Voisie* during the Middle Ages. Root: O. Fr. *envoisie* (the playful, mischievous one).

Vicar was a teasing nickname for an ancestor who walked about in a manner of "be as holy a person as I am". *Vicar* later became a respectable family name and is quite numerous in today's phone books.

Wallace see *Welsh*.

Welch see *Welsh*.

Welsh.   When a Welsh ancestor migrated from Wales, he was nicknamed *Welsh* or *Welch* in England, *Walsh* in Ireland and *Wallace* or *Wallis* in Scotland.   Root: A. S. *wealas* (stranger or foreigner).

Whelan was an Irish nickname for a youthful ancestor whose behavior was like a very frisky wolf pup. Root: Irish *faolain* (wolf).

The boastful Irish ancestor sometimes was nicknamed *Wherrity*,   Root: Irish *fagbartach* (the boaster).

37

An ancestor who has a skilled *Whistler* was readily so nicknamed. Root: O.E. *hwistlere*. This name is an occasional phonebook listing.

The ancestor who was the son of a widow was identified as *Widdowson*, from the Old English *widuwe*. Although it was a frequent nickname in medieval times, *Widdowson* does not have many listings in today's phone books.

Wilde and *Wilder* are frequent phonebook nickname listings, identifying the ancestor whose behavior was often outrageous and even dangerous. Root: O.E. *wilde*.

Wilder see *Wilde*.

Winter(s) nicknamed the ancestor born in the cold season of the year. Root: O.E. *winter*.

Wise. People is all centuries have indicated admiration for the ancestors who were learned and very intelligent. From the Old English *wis* (wise one), we got today's phone book nicKnames of *Wise*, *Wishard*, *Wiseman*, *Wisman*, and *Wyse*.

Wiseman see *Wise*.

Wishard see *Wise*.

Wren(n) was a nickname for an active, can't-sit-still ancestor, identifying him with the busy, flitting-about manner of a brown and black feathered farm-yard wren bird. Root: O.E. *wrenne*. *Wrenn* is the more frequent spelling in Britain.

Wyse see *Wise*.

- SOME ANCIENT NICKNAMES -

Years before the Norman French invaded England, nicknames of Celtic and Anglo-Saxon warrior supermen included:

Cadwallader (battle Hero)
Cuthbert (noble chieftain)
Egbert (brilliant swordsman)
Cedric (daring leader)

By 1910 A.D. American cartoonists used these ancient herioic names to portray "sissified" characters. The above thick-sounding syllables created humorous silhouettes of long ago "men of might and main". These once famous names soon disappeared from U.S.A. baptismal lists.

- ROBIN HOOD -

Robin Hood is the most famous nickname in English history. The Robin Hood tales have many earthy nicknames, giving us a word-picture of Robin Hood and his Merrymen (outlaws), as well as an insight into to the kind of folksy humor enjoyed in the Middle Ages.

Robin Hood - robber who always wore a green hood
Will Scarlet - always dressed in scarlet (red)
Little John - the giant-sized John
Ket the Troll - the dwarf-sized peasant
Reynold Grenelefe - wore a wrap of bright green
    cloth
Alan a'Dale - once lived in a valley (dalo)

Hob o'the Hill - Hob was a nickname for Rob; Hob
    always slept in a mound of earth
Diccon Cruikshanks - crooked-legs Dick
Peter the Quack - the duck-voiced archer
Luke the Red - the red-faced innkeeper
Sir Echo of the Harelip - nobleman with a mis-
    shapen lip
Lob-Lie-by-the-Fire - Lob the loafer
Cogg the Earless - the one-eared sailor
Lord Mumblemouth - the stuttering nobleman
Giles Crookleg - Giles the crippled yeoman
Grame Gapetooth - the forester with a missing
    tooth
Sir Richard Malbete - the cruel knight
Captain-Beat-The-Bush - the hunter of bush birds
Old Bat The Bandy - bow-legged Bartholomew

- PERSONAL APPEARANCE NICKNAMES -

Personal appearance nicknames were popular in the
Middle Ages, the recipient being easily identifiable
from amongst his or her family members or gather-
ings of townspeople. Sources for nicknames
included: unusual size or shape of the body, bald
heads, facial differences, deformities, and com-
parisons with birds. Nicknames also were used to
differentiate or compare people: whether they were
fat or thin, tall or short, dark or light skin, young
or old.

Throughout the ages cute infants have always been
admired. The influx of Flemish immigrants into
England in the late twelfth century introduced their
vernacular use of *quin* (kin). By 1300 A.D. the
suffix "kin" was frequently added to a cute young-
ster's name: *Dawkin(s)*, *Hawkin(s)*, *Simkin(s)*,
Watkin(s), *Perkin(s)*, *Hopkin(s)*, *Atkin(s)*,
Tomkin(s), etc. The final "s" identified the child
as "son of -- ". Kin was used almost exclusively
by the English lower classes.

Arlott was an uncomplimentary nickname for a young
beggar or scoundrel.

40

Armstrong was a complimentary nickname for a person that was strong of arm.

Auld see *Elder*.

From the Scottish *ban* (bones, bony) we have today's *Baines*, identifying a skinny person.

Ballard was an uncomplimentary nickname for a bald-headed person.

Bannon see *White*.

Bay(es) see *Red*.

Baynes see *White*.

Beard was a popular medieval nickname for ancestors with bushy or lengthy beards of black, red, white, or gray. Root: O. Fr. *barbe* (beard).

Beste was an uncomplimentary nickname for the beast-like person.

Very fat men were often labeled *Bigge(s)*, from the Old English *bigge*. See *Broad*.

Bird see *Byrd*.

Bissett see *Brown*.

Black was a nickname for a person of black hair or very dark skin. Root: O.E. *blaec*.

41

Blacket (Eng.)
Blackett (Eng.)
Blacklock (Eng.)
Blackman (Eng.)
Blackmon (Eng.)
Blackmun (Eng.)
Blackson (Eng.)
Blake (Scot.)
Blakeman (Scot.)
Blalock (Eng.)
Blaylock (Eng.)
Cole (Eng.)
Coles (Eng.)
Coleson (Eng.)
Darke (Eng.)
Dolan (Ir.)

Donne (Scot.)
Doud (Ir.)
Dow (Ir.)
Dowdy (Ir.)
Duffin (Ir.)
Dunne (Scot.)
Fitz Maurice (Ir.)
Fitz Morris (Ir.)
Maurice (Ir.)
Moore (Scot.)
Morrell (Eng.)
Morrice (Eng.)
Morrill (Eng.)
Morrin (Eng.)
Morris (Wel.)
Morrison (Wel.)

BLACK as a family name (nickname) in Europe today:

Chernoff - (Russ.)
Cherov - (Russ.)
Czarnecki - (Pol.)
Czerny - (Czech.)
Fekete - (Hun.)

Karas - (Greece)
Moreau - (Fr.)
Morena - (Ital., Span.)
Mustanen - (Finn.)
Swartz - (Ger.)

Blacket(t) see *Black.*

Blacklock see *Black.*

Blackman, *Blackmon*, *Blackmun* see *Black.*

Blackson see *Black.*

Blake(man) see *Black.*

Bla(y)lock see *Black.*

Blanchard see *White.*

Bland see *White.*

Blondell see *White.*

Blount see *White.*

Blundall, Blundell see *White.*

Blythe was a complimentary nickname for a fun-loving person.

Boyd see *White.*

Broad, from the Old English *brad,* identified a fat fellow as did *Bigge(s).*

Broadhead an English nickname for a person with a large or misshapened head.

The ancestor with a very *brad* or *bigge* "rear end" or "backside" was tormented as *Broadus* (broad arse).

Bronson see *Brown.*

Broun see *Brown.*

Brown is a nickname for a person of dark skin or brown hair. *Brown* was the most frequently used "color" nickname during the Middle Ages. Today *Brown* as a family name usually ranks among the ten most frequent names in U.S.A. telephone books. Root: O.E. *brun.*

Bissett (Scot.)	Carey (Ir.)
Bronson (Eng.)	Crone (Ir.)
Broun (Scot.)	Cronin (Ir.)
Browne (Eng.)	Deagan (Ir.)
Brownell (Eng.)	Dineen (Ir.)
Browning (Eng.)	Donegan (Ir.)
Brownson (Eng.)	Galbraith (Scot.)
Brunson (Eng.)	MacDougall (Scot., Ir.)
Burnett (Eng.)	Sorrell (Eng.)

Browne(ll) see *Brown.*

Browning see *Brown.*

Buck is from the Old English *bucca* (male goat) and identified an ancestor who was unpredictable as a male wild goat, or an ancestor who was as speedy as a male deer.

Bullitt an English nickname for a person with a large or misshapened head.

Bunche identified the hunchbacked ancestor. Root: O.E. *bunshe* (hunchback).

Bunyan, from the Old French *beugne* (bunion or knob), was a Middle Ages nickname for an ancestor with a lump, growth, or swelling on the face, foot, or hand.

Burnett see *Brown*.

Byrd was an uncomplimentary nickname for the person with bird-like mannerisms. *Byrd* and *Bird* are found in long lists in U.S.A. phonebooks, with *Byrd* almost three times more common as a family name than *Bird*. Is it a good guess that this nickname identified the ancestor who might quickly and silently disappear from sight as only a bird can do?

Caddick, from the Norman-French *caduc* (the feeble fellow), identified an epileptic or frail ancestor.

Caddock see *Caddick*.

The ancestor with a knobby growth on his face often was crudely nicknamed *Cade*. Root: O.E. *cade* (small barrel or cask), suggesting that this ancestor's face resembled a cask with a large plug or cork.

Caley was an Irish nickname for a skinny ancestor. Root: Irish *cael* (bony one).

Callow, from the Old English *calu-wig* (bald-headed warrior), was the term used in southwestern England to identify a bald person.

Calloway see *Callow*.

Calvin, from the Old Welsh *coluin* (bald), was the term used in western England to identify a bald person. *Calvin* was also a Roman nickname for "the hairless" infant.

An early Scottish ancestor with a hooked nose had the nickname of *Cameron*. Root: Gaelic *cam* (crooked) and *shron* (nose).

Camm was an uncomplimentary nickname for a cross-eyed person.

Cammel see *Campbell*.

Campbell is from the Gaelic *cam* (crooked) and *beul* (mouth), nicknaming the "crooked mouth" or deceitful Scottish ancestor. *Cammell* is a much later English version.

Carey, from the Irish *ciardha* meaning "the dark one". See *Brown*.

Cecil was a Roman nickname for "the blind one (infant)".

Chaffe, from the Norman-French *chauff* (bald), was the term used in northeastern England to identify a bald person.

Chaffin see *Chaffe*.

Cheeks was a nickname for an ancestor with an oversized jaw and puffy cheeks. Root: O.E. *ceace* (cheeks).

A plump ancestor risked being labeled *Chubb*. Root: O.E. *chubbe* (a dull-eyed fat fish).

Claude was a Roman nickname for "the misshapen or crippled" child.

Cole, Coles, Coleson see *Black.*

Colvin see *Calvin.*

Corbett identified the ancestor with raven-black hair. Root: O. Fr. *corbet.*

Corbin see *Corbett.*

Crabbe identified the very short ancestor from southwestern England whose slow walking style suggested the movement of a crab. *Crabbe* also was an uncomplimentary nickname for a nasty-tempered person in London district. Root: O.E. *crabbe.*

Crain was an American variation of *Crane.*

The skinny, long-legged crane bird was a common sight in England, particularly in marshy, wetland places. It was easy to nickname a skinny, long-legged person as *Crane.* Root: O.E. *cran.*

Cratchet nicknamed the lame person who walked with the aid of crutches (as did Tim Cratchet in Dickens' <u>A</u> <u>Christmas</u> <u>Carol</u>). Root: O.E. *crucche* (crutch).

Crimmins see *Cummings.*

Cripps see *Curley.*

Crisp(in) see *Curley.*

Critchet see *Cratchet.*

Crockett identified an ancestor with a lame or crooked leg. Root: O.E. *crocod.*

Crone see *Brown.*

Cronen, from the Irish *cronain* meaning "the dark-faced one".

Cronin see *Brown.*

Crookshanks see *Cruikshanks.*

An Irish hunchbacked ancestor could have been named *Crotty*. Root: Irish *crotach* (humpbacked one).

The ancestor with shining black hair was quickly named *Crowe.*

Crowell see *Crowe.*

Cruilshanks was the Scottish label for a lame ancestor. Root: Scot. *cruik* (crooked) and *shanks* (legs). *Crookshanks* was a much later version.

Crump see *Cummings.*

Cummings identified the Scottish ancestor who walked in a bent over position. Root: Scot. *cuimin* (bent over).

Curley, from the Old French *crespe* (curly-haired), was the nickname for a curly-haired person.

Darke see *Black.*

Deagan see *Brown.*

Dineen see *Brown.*

Dolan see *Black.*

Donegan see *Brown.*

Donne see *Black.*

Doty see *Doughty.*

Doud see *Black.*

Medieval men were quick to admire and praise the ancestor of great strength and physical endurance, nicknaming such as man *Doughty*. Root: O.E. *dohti* (strong one).

Dove identified "the gentle one". Root: O.E. *dufe.*

Dow(dy) see *Black.*

Drake ridiculed the ancestor who waddle-walked like a duck. Root: O.E. *draca* (male duck).

Duffin see *Black.*

Dunne see *Black.*

Elder was a complimentary nickname for an older, senior person.

Fairchild was a complimentary nickname for the handsome young man.

Fairfax see *White.*

A hawk-nosed (hooked nose) or cunning person was sometimes nicknamed *Falcon*, from the Old French *faucon* (falcon).

Fayer see *White.*

The ancestor who was "as frisky and fussy as a finch in a cage" easily would have been labeled *Finch*. Root: O.E. *finc* (finch).

FitzMaurice see *Black.*

FitzMorris see *Black.*

Floyd see *Lloyd*.

Flynn see *Red*.

It's a good guess that the name of *Foote* once was an uncomplimentary nickname for an ancestor with a misshapen or lame foot. Root: O.E. *fot*.

Frost see *White*.

Gainer see *White*.

Galbraith see *Brown*.

Galligan see *White*.

Galvin see *White*.

Gammon poked fun at the ancestor with a shortened leg. Root: O. Fr. *jambe* (leg).

Gaynor see *White*.

Gittings identified the Welsh ancestor of sloppy appearance.

Gooch see *Red*.

Gough see *Red*.

Grant identified the ancestor who was a tall, large man. Root: Norman French *grande* (large).

49

Gray was a nickname for a person with gray hair. Root: O.E. *graeg.*

Grey (Eng.)	Grissin (Eng.)
Grice (Eng.)	Grissom (Eng.)
Griss (Eng.)	Hoare (Eng.)
Grissen (Eng.)	Lloyd (Wel.)
	Loyd (Wel.)

Grice see *Gray.*

Griss(en), Grissin see *Gray.*

Grissom see *Gray.*

Grosscup was an American nickname for a person with a large or misshapened head. Root: Ger. *groskopf* (oversized head).

Gwinn see *White.*

Gwynn(e) is from the Welsh *gwynn* (light-colored hair or skin). Also spelled *Wynn.*

Gynn see *White.*

Hawk(e) nicknamed "the cruel one". Root: O.E. *hafec.*

Head was an English nickname for a person with a large or misshapened head.

A long-legged, bony peasant often was named after the *Heron* bird of similar leg structure. Root: O.E. *heroune* (heron).

Hoare see *Gray.*

Kavanaugh, from the Irish root *caomhanaigh*, identified the Irishman who was "handsome and kindly".

A skinny Irish ancestor was nicknamed *Kealey* (*Keeley*), from the Irish *caollaidhe* (thin one).

Keeley see *Kealey*.

Keir was a frequent nickname for a black-haired Scottish ancestor. Root: Gaelic *ciar* (black).

Kennedy was an Irish nickname for a person with a large or misshapened head. Root: Irish *cinneide* (large head).

Kilroy see *Red*.

Kyte identified the person who was "as vicious as a kite bird". Root: O.E. *cyta*.

Ladd identified "the youthful" ancestor. Root: O.E. *ladda*.

Why do we say it? Near the end of the fifteenth century it was the custom of British royalty to avoid a whipping punishment for a young prince since the lad was deemed to be as inviolable as his father. A youth was selected to be playmate and pupil for the prince.

Such a playmate was teased as "somebody's whipping boy," for the playmate received a flogging whenever the prince deserved stern punishment.

By the end of the nineteenth century British royalty eliminated this custom of a "whipping boy" in the palace. The phrase became a part of general speech over the centuries for anyone who is blamed and punished for an action he or she never committed.

Laing see *Lang*.

Lang(e) and *Laing* were Scottish nicknames for a tall person.

Langan was an Irish nickname for a tall person.

Lange see *Lang*.

Little, *Littell*, *Lytle*, and *Lyttle* identified the small ancestor.

Littlejohn was the complimentary nickname for the giant-sized John (see *Robin Hood*).

Lloyd, from the Gaelic *llwyd*. *Lloyd* was often pronounced *Floyd* in England. See *Gray*.

Long, *Longfellow*, and *Longman* were English nicknames for a tall person.

Loyd see *Gray*.

Lyt(t)le see *Little*.

MacDougall is *Brown* in Scottish and Irish.

Maurice is from the Norman-French *maurice* meaning "the moor or dark-faced one". See *Black*.

A mocking nickname for the youthful plump person was *Metcalfe*. ROOT: O.E. *mete-calf* (fatted calf).

Milligan poked fun at the "small bald fellow". Root: Irish *maoileagain*.

Many *Mitchells* are listed in today's phone books. This nickname identified "the very large fellow". Root: O.E. *mycel* (big, large).

Moore see *Black*.

Morrell see *Black.*

Morrice see *Black.*

Morrill see *Black.*

Morrin see *Black.*

Morris(on) see *Black.*

Morse see *Black.*

Moylan was an Irish nickname for a bald-headed ancestor. Root: Irish *maol.*

Munn was a complimentary nickname for a person who had a face like a monk's.

Paddock was a Scottish nickname for an ancestor with frog-like features. Root: *paddue* (frog).

A *Parrot*-nosed ancestor was a ready-made victim for a nickname. Root: O. Fr. *perot* (parrott).

Partridge compared the plump-sized ancestor to his or her bird namesake. Root: O.E. *partriche.*

Peacock was a fitting comparison for a strutting, "show-off" ancestor. Root: O.E. *peacocc.*

Pigge identified the pig-like individual.

- - - - - - - - - -

Why do we say PIGGY BANK? During the twelfth and thirteenth centuries English housewives saved small coins in a small clay jar called a *pygg.* It was so named because this jar was usually make from a low-grade clay called *pygg* clay. By the eighteenth century British potters made pig shaped coin holders to encourage

53

children to save money. By the twentieth century any shape of such a coin
box was called a PIGGY BANK.

- - - - - - - - - -

The ancestor whose hair always looked like the
head of a mop was sometimes nicknamed *Quigley*,
from the Irish *coigligh* (the shaggy-headed one).

Read(e) see *Red*.

Red was a nickname for a person of red hair or
complexion. Root: O.E. *read*.

Bay (Eng.)
Bayes (Eng.)
Flynn (Ir.)
Gooch (Wel., Ir.)
Gough (Ir.)
Kilroy (Ir.)
Read (Eng.)
Reade (Eng.)
Redd (Eng.)

Rede (Eng.)
Reed (Eng.)
Reid (Scot.)
Rouse (Eng., Fr.)
Rudd (Eng.)
Ruff (Eng.)
Russ (Eng.)
Russell (Eng.)
Rust (Scot., Eng.)

Reed, *Reid* see *Red*.

Rouse see *Red*.

Rudd see *Red*.

Ruff see *Red*.

Russ(ell) see *Red*.

Rust see *Red*.

The ancestor with curly, crisp hair was admired as
Scripps. Root: O. Fr. *crespe* (crisp).

Smollett was an uncomplimentary Scottish nickname
for a person with a small head. Root: O.E. *smael*
(small) and *heafod* (head).

54

Snow see *White.*

Sorrell see *Brown.*

Jack Spratt (who could eat no fat) may have been nicknamed *Spratt* because his thin face suggested the face of a *sprat* (a small fish). Root: O.E. *sprotte.*

Stearns see *Stern(e).*

Stern(e) or *Stearns* nicknamed the serious-faced ancestor. Root: O.E. *styrne* (grim-faced one). *Stern(e)* has many more phone book listings than *Stearns.*

Strang was the Scottish variation of *Armstrong.*

Swift was a complimentary nickname for the fast runner.

Tait nicknamed the ancestor who had a large, or misshapen head. Root: O. Fr. *tete* (head).

Tate is the American version of *Tait.*

Topp(er) was a sort of cartoon-name for the ancestor with a peculiar "straight-up" clump of hair that was noticeable even at a distance. Root: O.E. *toppe* (clump).

The village greens of England were places for two favorite medieval sports: bow-and-arrow competitions, and games and athletic feats, which often required brute strength. Only a bull-sized fellow might be able to grab a bull's head and turn the animal completely around, earning this giant-sized man the enviable nickname of *Turnbull.*

The dignified sound of *Vaughan* was a nickname for a short person. Root: Welsh *fychan* (shorty).

White was a nickname for a person of light complexion or hair. Root: O.E. *hwit.*

Bannon (Ir.)
Baynes (Eng.)
Blanchard (Eng.)
Bland (Eng.)
Blondell (Eng.)
Blount (Eng.)
Blundall (Eng.)
Blundell (Eng.)
Boyd (Ir.)
Fairfax (Eng.)
Fayer (Eng.)
Frost (Eng.)
Gainer (Ir.)

Galligan (Ir.)
Galvin (Ir.)
Gaynor (Ir.)
Gwinn (Wel.)
Gynn (Wel.)
Snow (Eng.)
Whitehead (Eng.)
Whitman (Eng.)
Whitset (Eng.)
Whitson (Eng.)
Whitt (Eng.)
Whyte (Eng.)

Whit(t)ed is an English variation of *White*.

Whitehead see *White*.

Whiteman is an English variation of *White*.

Whitlock is an English variation of *White*.

Whitman see *White*.

Whitset, *Whitson* see *White*.

Whitt see *White*.

Whitten is an English variation of *White*.

Whyte see *White*.

Winne is a Welsh variation of *White*.

Witte is an English variation of *White*.

Wittman is an English variation of *White*.

Wynn see *Gwynn*.

Wynne is a Welsh variation of *White*.

Young is a much listed nickname in our phone books, probably identifying almost 400,000 *Youngs* in America. It was spelled *Yonge* in medieval times. *Younger(s)* and *Youngman* are variations. In most cases *Young* identified "the younger of two men" (son and father). Root: O.E. *yonge*.

Younger(s) see *Young*.

Youngman see *Young*.

CHAPTER 4

15% of our FAMILY NAMES come from OCCUPATIONS

We often identify people by mentioning their occupations. We say "the dry cleaner", "the mailman", "the preacher", or "the plumber". Our ancestors also identified persons by their occupations.

Some female workers in the Middle Ages often had occupational names that were slightly different from male workers who did the same kind of work. The difference was the addition of "ster" to the occupation name.

MALE worker	FEMALE worker
Aleman (ale server)	Alester
Baker	Bakester (Baxter)
Dyer (of cloth)	Dyster (Dexter)
Hawker (pedlar)	Hawkster (huckster)
Seamer (tailor)	Seamster
Spinner (of cloth)	Spinster
Webber (weaver of cloth)	Webster

- CASTLES and OCCUPATIONAL NAMES -

A twelfth or thirteenth century castle was a fortress that usually was located on high ground near a stream. Such an elevated site made it difficult for an enemy to attack and the river provided the necessary supply of water for the fortress. Many workers were required to provide the variety of services for the daily routines in castle life.

Castles in Britain were built of wood before the Norman-French conquered the country in 1066 A.D. The Normans introduced the use of stone for palaces and churches. Bricks were used by 1350 A.D. in order to give variety and style to the outside walls of a building or house. The use of stone greatly reduced the menace of fire that occurred often in earlier wooden castles.

Floors in medieval days were usually plain earth, and they were cleaned by a quick scraping and sweeping of such ground surface. Royalty and noblemen often used rugs of fur. Poor persons made coarse straw mats for winter use when their earthen floors often became frozen.

The common castle day began at sunrise. The crowing of roosters in the castle courtyard were the daily alarm clocks. The lord of the estate was awakened by his page who helped the nobleman to dress. Soon the chapel bell rang for the noble family to attend early morning prayer. Since it was a medieval custom to have only two meals a day, breakfast was served about 10:00 a.m.

When a castle meal was finished, one or more pages were ordered to "clear the table" - a table much like today's ping pong tables. The table top and its X-supports or legs could be stacked against a wall.

Today's many family names ending in "man" still remind us of a long ago ancestor and his occupation:

> *Beaman* - bee keeper
> *Bellman* - bellringer
> *Bowerman* - chamber servant
> *Buckman* - goat herder
> *Chapman* - peddler
> *Chessman* - cheese maker
> *Dickman* - ditch digger

Fishman - fish seller
Inman - inn worker
Tubman - barrel maker
Waterman - boat worker

Family names ending in "s" as in *Dukes*, *Mills*, *Parsons*, *Masters*, and *Vickers* often identified:

the duke's servant   the master's servant
the miller's servant   the vicar's servant
the parson's servant

Archer identified the soldier who was skilled with a bow and arrow. It also identified a maker of bows and arrows. Root: Fr. *archier* (bowman). See *Ballaster* and *Gossard*.

- - - - - - - - - -

> The crossbow of the Middle Ages was more powerful than the English longbow. However, a longbow archer could shoot four arrows for every single crossbow arrow shot. The crossbow was invented in Italy in the eleventh century. A longbow (generally made of yew wood) usually measured six feet high and shot arrows of a yard in length.
>
> In the Middle Ages yew boughs (evergreen branches) were fastened above a doorway as a symbol of sorrow (death) in a family.

- - - - - - - - - -

Armour identified the ancestor who made and repaired armor. Medieval warriors used spears, axes, and swords to lengthen the power of the human arm. Most large castles stored weapons in an armory with the armourer as its custodian. Root: Fr. *armourier* (armourer). See *Armstead*.

61

Armstead was another medieval name for an armory. See *Armour*. Root: O.E. *stede* (station or place), identifying the place where armour and arms were stored.

Bachelor. In 1250 A.D. a "bachelor" was a youthful aristocrat who was in training to become a knight. By 1500 A.D. a bachelor identified an unmarried man who was a university graduate. *Batchelor* was the spelling in Scotland. *Batchelder* was a later variation. Root: O.Fr. *bachelor* (young aristocrat).

Ballaster identified a crossbowman warrior or maker of crossbows. The crossbow was a fifteenth century weapon, invented in Italy, and it shot steel arrows. Root: O. Fr. *arbalastier* (crossbowman). Also spelled *Ballister*. See *Archer*, *Quarrell*.

Barber. Barbers in medieval Britain were hair and beard trimmers, surgeons, dentists, and blood-letters (a vein was opened in hope of improving a health condition. Robin Hood died from such a treatment). *Barbour* is a variation. Root: Fr. *barbier*.

Bode identified a medieval messenger or herald, an important type of service in the Middle Ages. Root: O.E. *boda* (messenger).

Bower(s) is a variation of *Bowman*. See *Archer*.

Bowman. Root: O.E. *boga* (bow). See *Archer*.

Bowyer is a variation of *Bowman*. See *Archer*.

Boyer is a variation of *Bowman*. See *Archer*.

Brenner identified the trainer and keeper of the castle dogs. Brave hunting dogs were as highly prized as were horses, for much of a nobleman's time was spent in hunting. In most hunts the dogs cornered a beast then the men attacked the encircled beast, using swords and spears to kill the game they had chased. Root: O. Fr. *bernier* (kennel keeper).

Brisbane was an occupational nickname for the castle prison torturer (the bone breaker). He was not a popular fellow worker. Root: O. Fr. *brise* (to break) and *bane* (bone).

- - - - - - - - - -

During the Middle Ages criminals often were burned at the stake. Such an execution was known as a "bone fire". Over the centuries bone fire changed into today's happier experience of "bonfire".

- - - - - - - - - -

Butler identified the person in charge of the wine pantry or cellar (the bottler). Root: O. Fr. *bouteil-lier* (wine servant).

Carnall see *Carnell*.

Carnell identified a bowman's battle station at a castle wall. Root: O. Fr. *crenel* (an opening through which an archer shot arrows at castle attackers.) *Carnall* is a variation.

Carter identified the operator of a hand cart or driver of two-wheel cart pulled by one or more oxen. Root: O. Fr. *charetier* (charioteer). (By the

63

eleventh century a new type of harness for oxen and horses had been invented, enabling such animals to pull loads heavier than what could be carried in a two-wheeled cart.)

Castle(man) identified the ancestor who worked and lived in a castle. Root: O.E. *castel* (castle).

Catching(s) see *Ketchen.*

Chalmers is Scottish for *Chamberlain.*

Chamberlain identified the person in charge of the king's or lord's private apartment. *Chalmers* is the Scottish version. Root: Fr. *chamberlain.*

Chambers see *Chamberlain.*

Chaplin identified the castle minister in charge of its shrine or chapel. Root: O. Fr. *chapelain* (chaplain).

Chase identified the ancestor whose task was to organize the frequent, elaborate castle hunting parties. *Chase* usually lived in a hut at the entrance to the castle forest. Today a *Chase* would be known as a hunting guide. Root: O. Fr. *chaceur* (hunter).

Chevalier identified a warrior servant to a king, lord, or a knight. Root: O. Fr. *chevalier* (horseman).

The *Cook* prepared food in the castle kitchen. Root: O.E. *cueccan* (to cook). In a large castle the kitchen would have two fireplaces with cranes and spits for roasting two or three pigs or one-quarter of cow or bull. The kitchen employed several servants to assist the cook.

Cushman identified the maker of protective leather or metal leg armor. He was a special craftsman, for such leg armor had to be made by exact measurement of the upper and lower parts of the leg. Root: O. Fr. *cuisse* (thigh).

Drover identified the cattle herder. Root: O.E. *draf* (cattle herd).

Durward identified the door keeper for the large castle hall. Root: O.E. *duru* (door) and *weard* (guard).

Falconer identified the trainer and keeper of falcons, birds which the kings and lords used in the sport of hunting. *Falk*, *Falkner*, and *Faulkner* were later variations. A good falcon was valued as much as a prized horse or dog. Root: O. Fr. *fauconnier*.

Falk(ner) see *Falconer*.

Faulkner see *Falconer*.

Fowler identified the hunter of wild fowl. He used arrows with specially shaped points. A fowler also was skilled at trapping birds by the use of a net. The captured birds were placed in a cage where they remained until they were needed for a nobleman's dinner. Root: O.E. *fughelere* (fowler).

Galer see *Gaylor*.

Gandy identified the ancestor who was in charge of the castle gander (male geese) pens. Root: O.E. *gandra* (gander).

Gardener identified the ancestor who tended the castle gardens, cultivating shrubbery and flowers. Also spelled *Gerdner*. Root: O. Fr. *jardinier* (gardener).

Garner identified the ancestor who was in charge of the castle's grain storage bins. Root: O.Fr. *gernier* (graineryman).

Garson identified a male servant in the castle. Root: O. Fr. *garcon*.

Gates see *Yates*.

Gayler see *Gaylor*.

Gaylor identified a castle jailer who had all the keys to cells in the castle's large dungeon. Also spelled *Galer*, *Gayler*, and *Goaler*. Root: O. Fr. *jaiolier*.

Gerdner see *Gardener*.

Gilligan was an occupational nickname for a youthful servant in an Irish castle. Root: Gaelic *gille* (servant).

Goaler see *Gaylor.*

Gossard identified the ancestor who tended the geese flock. He supplied special goose feathers for arrows: three goose tail feathers of the same size were fitted to the tail of the arrow; these balanced an arrow on its way to a target. Root: O.E. *gos* (goose) and *hierde* (guardian).

Granger identified the supervisor of the castle's farm equipment and buildings. He decided when a field bridge needed repair or when sheep enclosures needed mending. Root: O. Fr. *graunge* (barn foreman).

Grosvenor. Medieval aristocrats preferred wild game over port or beef. The chief huntsman (grosvenor) had to provide deer, bear, rabbit, or boar meat (a special delicacy) for the castle menu. Root: O. Fr. *gros* (chief) and *veneur* (hunter).

Hallman. A medieval castle hall usually was large and able to contain two hundred or more persons. The hall was a place for the evening meal and for feasts, and a place where peasants could gather to ask for bread in times of famine. The *Hallman* was the servant whose duty was to prepare the hall for its various daily uses. Root: O.E. *heall* (hall).

- - - - - - - - - -

By 1400 A.D. English noblemen were hanging tapestries on the walls of castle halls. In earlier centuries Norman-French castle walls had been decorated with lances, shields, banners, and deer and boar skulls.

- - - - - - - - - -

Harper was a minstrel and story-teller who performed at evening meals and feasts. Root: O. Fr. *harpeor.*

67

Hayward see *Howard*.

Hirdman was a Scottish name for a herder of sheep or cattle. Root: O.E. *hierde* (herd).

Hines was an English occupational name for a servant who was "as timid as a hind" (a female red deer). Also spelled *Hynes*. Root: O.E. *hinde*.

Hoggarth identified the castle estate swine herder. Also spelled *Hoggard*. Root: O.E. *hogg* and *hierde* (herd).

Hornblower identified the ancestor who blew a horn at sunrise to awaken the servants for their daily routine. His hornblowing also announced the commencement of feasts, the arrival at the castle moat gate of special guests, and of the beginning of a fox or boar hunt. Root: O.E. *horna* and *blawere*.

Howard identified the ancestor whose duty was to round up stray cattle and who repaired hedges or other enclosures to prevent cattle from getting loose. He was also known as *Hayward*. Little Boy Blue was a "hayward" or "howard". Root: O.E. *how* (enclosure) and *ward* (keeper or guard).

Hunter see *Grosvenor*. Root: O.E. *huntian* (to hunt).

Hynes see *Hines*.

Jenner identified the ancestor "engineer" who made hurling machines that catapulted stones, thick arrows, and flaming torches at the enemy attacking a castle. Root: O. Fr. *engigneor* (engineer).

Jester identified the ancestor who provided entertainment in the castle hall. He was part clown, part fool, a practical joker, and a teller of humorous stories. Root: O. Fr. *geste*.

Ketchen. Because fire was a constant menace, the kitchen of a large abbey, manor, or castle was usually in a separate building with a covered passageway leading to the main hall where the dining occurred. Such a food preparation center had a dozen or more male and female serfs.

A kitchen had at least two large cooking hearths: one fireplace to prepare stews, soups, and vegetables and on the opposite side was an ample fireplace where a large roasting spit contained poultry, joints of beef or lamb, or a complete carcass. Today's family names from kitchen workers are: *Ketchen*, *Kichin*, *Kitchener*, *Kitching*, and *Catching(s)*. Root: O. Dan. *koppen* (to cook) and O.E. *cycene* (kitchen).

- - - - - - - - - -

The Normans introduced the French words of boeuf (beef), porc (pork), poule (poultry), and mouton (mutton) when they conquered England in 1066 A.D. Their Anglo-Saxon slaves labored from sunrise to sundown to raise steers (boeuf), pigs (porc), sheep (mouton), and chickens (poule) for their Norman-French lords and ladies. By 1150 A.D. these Anglo-Saxon word roots were used daily in most English households.

- - - - - - - - - -

Kichin see *Ketchen.*

Kitchener see *Ketchen.*

Kitching see *Ketchen.*

Knight identified the ancestor who functioned as an aristocratic servant to a king or an important lord of a large estate. He was unable to read or write, but he was usually very strong and courageous. A knight's chief skills were in battle, hunting, and tournament jousting. Root: O.E. *cniht* (knight).

Lardner identified the ancestor who was in charge of the larder or pantry (place where daily essential foods were stored.) In the castle larder were meats, cheese, varieties of peas and beans, cabbages, leeks, onions, beets, and turnips – all part of a meal's menu. Also in the castle larder were figs, peaches, apples, pears, wild berry and nut varieties. Root: O.E. *lardier* (pantry keeper). See *Spencer.*

Larimer see *Lorimer.*

Larrimore see *Lorimer.*

Leach was an occupational name for a medieval physician whose first treatment for most diseases was to bleed the patient. For this he used blood-sucking insects, worms, or a crude puncture instrument. Today's red-striped barber pole is a reminder that medieval barbers also were allowed to bleed patients. *Leech* and *Leitch* were later spellings. Root: A.S. *laece* (leech).

Leech see *Leach.*

Leitch see *Leach.*

Locke. The many doors, gates, cells, and chests in a palace required a special locksmith to repair or replace locks and lost keys. Root: O.E. *loc* (lock).

Lockhart identified the ancestor who tended castle animals in a small pen which held them until they were ready for slaughter in the courtyard. Root: O.E. *loc* (lock) and *hierde* (herder).

Lor(r)imer identified the medieval craftsmen who made special horse hardware including such items as spurs and bridles. By the eleventh century horse stirrups were in use; these were of great benefit for knights: stirrups reduced the risk of a warrior falling off a horse during combat. Also spelled *Larrimore* and *Larimer*. Root: O.E. *lorimer*.

Marshall identified a medieval horse expert who was responsible for the health and maintenance of a King's or nobleman's horses. Root: O.Fr. *mareschal*.

- - - - - - - - - -

By the eleventh century horseshoes were in use in Britain. Horseshoes greatly reduced the frequent lameness that these animals suffered. Wearing shoes, horses kept much better balance in bad weather.

- - - - - - - - - -

Mason. The medieval mason in a castle always had more work than he could handle. Weather conditions caused castle wall defects that had to be repaired at once to keep out rain or snow - or enemies. *Mayson* was a later spelling. Root: O. Fr. *macon*.

Mayson see *Mason*.

Miller identified the ancestor who was the castle grinder of grain. This is one of the oldest of occupational names. *Milne* and *Mil(l)ner* are medieval variations. *Millar* was a frequent Scottish spelling. Root: Latin *molendarius* (miller).

Millman identified the ancestor who was a miller's servant. See *Miller*.

Napier identified the ancestor who was responsible for the castle towels, drapes, blankets, and similar articles. Root: O. Fr. *nappe* (tablecloth).

Newhall identified the ancestor who worked in a new or rebuilt castle hall.

Norris see *Nourse*.

Nourse identified the ancestral woman who served as a nurse for the sick and who tended severely disabled persons in the castle. *Norris* is a variation. Root: O.E. *nurice*.

Padgett see *Page*.

Page identified a young attendant (servant) for the king or lord of the castle. He was the son of a nobleman. The page was sent to a castle at age ten or eleven to begin his training as a future knight. The page always accompanied his king or lord to a battlefront. *Padgett* and *Paget* were variations. Root: O. Fr. *paget* (page).

Paget see *Page*.

Pastor identified a baker of pastry in the castle kitchen. Root: O. Fr. *paste* (pastry).

Pinder identified the ancestor who was the medieval cowboy on the castle estate. His task was to round up stray animals roaming the estate. Root: O.E. *pyndar* (cattle catcher).

Plater identified the ancestor who worked in the castle armory where he shaped plates of metal to

72

make suits of armor for knights and horses. The head, chest, and flanks of a horse needed protection from arrow shots or spear thrusts. Root: O. Fr. *plate*.

Porter identified the ancestor with a strong back for carrying heavy loads. Root: O. Fr. *porteur*.

Portman identified the ancestor who served as a doorman to the king's or lord's private apartment. Root: O. Fr. *porte* (door).

Potter identified the medieval craftsman who made various kitchen pots, dining plates, and goblets.

Pottinger identified the ancestor who made soup or "pottage" in a castle or plantation kitchen. Peasants and soldiers at a castle or plantation were usually served a heavy soup made from leftover meat scraps and bones cooked with barley or beans. Sometimes the soup consisted of fish scraps and leftover cooked vegetables. Root: O. Fr. *pottage* (soup).

Quarrell identified the ancestor who made the heavy, steel arrows for the cross-bow. Such arrows usually had square tips. Root: O. Fr. *quarrel* (square arrow tip). See *Ballaster*.

Reeve(s). A medieval reeve was the peasant foreman for other peasants (serfs). The reeve supervised farm tasks of his fellow serfs: the ploughing of their strips of land, the collection and use of animal manure, their method of harvesting grain, and their digging of irrigation ditches. Root: O.E. *refa* (foreman or boss).

Rider and *Ryder* identified the horseman guardian of the castle woods. He patrolled the forest in search of "poachers" (peasants who caught fish or trapped animals illegally in the estate woods). Punishment for poaching was barbaric: a peasant's right hand was chopped off. For a second offense he was hanged from a castle wall. Root: O.E. *ridere* (rider).

Roebuck identified the ancestor who was an expert at trapping roebucks (male deer). He also taught young castle aristocrats the skill of deer hunting. Root: O.E. *ra* (red) and *bucc* (male animal).

Sadler was an expert medieval saddlemaker who was highly valued by a king or lord. Kings and noblemen had as much pride for a good saddle and riding horse as we have for a good automobile. Knights preferred highly ornamental saddles which were eventually handed on to a son or nephew. (During the Middle Ages a white or gray horse was the Rolls Royce of horses.) Root: O.E. *sadol* (saddle).

Sargent identified the ancestor who was a military attendant to a knight. Root: O. Fr. *sergent*.

Shields identified the ancestor who made shields for knights and soldiers. The Anglo-Saxon shield was always round. The Norman-French shield was egg-shaped with the small part of the "egg" at the bottom; the upper and wider part protected the face

74

and body. French shields were lighter to carry in battle than those of the Anglo-Saxons'.

- - - - - - - - - -

Why do we say "buckle down to work?" In the Middle Ages when an English soldier was preparing himself for action, he very carefully buckled his shield to his arm. Through nine hundred years of English language, "get ready to fight" changed to today's "get ready to work".

- - - - - - - - - -

Spear and *Spier* identified the ancestor who was a lookout high in a castle tower, spying out on the surrounding countryside for any large, approaching group of horsemen. See *Wakeman.*

Spencer was an occupational name for a lardner. See *Lardner.* Root: O. Fr. *despensier* (a dispenser). Also spelled *Spenser.*

Spier see *Spear.*

Steward identified the ancestor who was a steward for a royal or nobleman's estate. He was a nobleman who managed the property of royalty or aristocracy. The Norman-French *Stuart* name came to Britain with William the Conqueror in 1066 A.D. *Stuart* and *Steward* are very common Scottish family names. Root: O.E. *stow* (place of a palace or hall) and *weard* (manager and protector).

Stuart see *Steward.*

Trotter identified the ancestor who was a castle messenger. Root: O. Fr. *trotier* (a trotter).

Trout(man) identified an ancestor who caught fish for the castle meals. Root: O.E. *truht* (trout).

Venner see *Grosvenor*.

Waite identified the ancestor who worked as a fire watchman within a large castle, carrying a horn to blow in case of fire. Also spelled *Wayte*. Root: O.Fr. *gwaite* (guard).

Wakeman identified a tower lookout. A *Wakeman* blew his horn at sunrise to awaken castle workers or to warn of a fire in the castle. The threat and menace of fire in a castle was greatly feared. Soon after sunset the castle watchman blew a horn to remind everyone to put out the fires in the various chamber fireplaces, a safety procedure that the Norman-French brought to Britain called *couvre feu* (smother the fire). This is how we got today's word "curfew" for "lights out". See *Spear*.

Wayte see *Waite*.

Yates identified the operator and tender of the castle moat gates. Root: O.E. *geat*.

Yeatman and *Yeats* are Irish variations for *Yates*.

Youngman identified the youthful servant. During the twelfth century many castle tasks could be inherited. Thus a servant might be identified as "youngman (son of) chamberlin," "youngman (son of) barber," "youngman (son of) falconer," etc. Root: O.E. *younge* (young).

- OCCUPATION NAMES from
TOWN PEOPLE and CHURCH WORKERS -

In the center of a medieval town was a large, open-air space used as a daily market where fruits and vegetables and other kinds of merchandise were sold.

The town streets were narrow and crooked. Most houses were required by law to have a stone foundation as a means of fire prevention. All craft workers had their shops at ground level and they lived in rooms above the shops.

The market square was the town center of activities. Here stood the town hall and the town cathedral. Festival and religious plays occurred in the town market place.

A Middle Ages town usually had high, thick walls (at least four feet thick) with a high gate which was opened at sunrise and closed at sunset. These thick, high walls and gates were protection against robber gangs and packs of wild animals that appeared after nightfall.

Bailey identified the ancestor who had a special legal responsibility. In Scotland he was the chief judge (*Bailie*) in a district. In English regions he served as deputy sheriff (*Bailey*) for several districts; or as the chief lawman for a very large manor. In Norman-French times the "bailey" was in charge of a castle's outer wall. His task was to keep this wall difficult to penetrate by attack. Root: O. Fr. *balie* (bailey).

Bailie see *Bailey*.

Bellman identified the ancestor who rang church bells - or he may have been a town crier who announced important news as he walked the streets of a town. He often clanged a hand bell to announce his presence. Root: O.E. *belle*.

- - - - - - - - - -

Why do we say "o'clock"? In the later Middle Ages many town bell towers announced the hour of the day. By the fourteenth century an English person was saying, "It's now ten of the clock." By the end of the seventeenth century time-telling became shortened to plain "o'clock" (ten

77

o'clock).   Root: O. Fr. *cloche*
(clawk).

- - - - - - - - - -

Biddle identified the ancestor who usually served as
a kind of courtroom policeman or village authority
for law and order. Root: O.E. *bvdel*. *Beadle* or
Bedel were Middle Ages spellings.

Bishop identified the person who as a bishop – or
who worked in a bishop's manor. If an ancestor
acted the part of a bishop in a religious festival
year after year, he usually was nicknamed "bishop".
Root: O.E. *bisceop* (bishop).

Bridge(s) and *Bridgeman* identified the ancestor who
collected a toll from travelers crossing the bridge.
Root: *brycg* (bridge).

Cannon identified an ancestor who served as a minister within a cathedral. Root: O.E. *canoun* (cannon).

Catcher.   Fear and contempt for tax collectors
marched alongside progress in the parade of history
through the centuries. The medieval taxman inquired
about poultry, animal hides, stored grains, and the
like for assessment and tax collection.   A tax-
gatherer for an abbey would circle the large
religious estate with a caged cart in which he collected loose animals, poultry, and other goods when
he could not collect the tax in silver. *Cachier* was
the Old French "catcher" or "chaser" of taxes.
Variations include: *Catchpole* (poultry chaser or
catcher) and *Ketcher*.

Catchpole see *Catcher*.

Chancellor identified the ancestor who kept the
records of a court of law. He was held in high esteem in his town because he was able to read and
write. Root: O.E. *chanceler*.

78

Chapman identified the ancestor who was a peddler that traveled from town to town. He walked the town's streets yelling, "Cheapman's here! Cheapman's here!" *Chatman* and *Chipman* were other variations for this peddler with cheap merchandise. Root: O.E. *ceap* (cheap).

Chatman see *Chapman*.

Chipman see *Chapman*.

Church(ward) identified the ancestor who worked in a church on a non-clergyman basis. A *Churchward* was the warden or guard of church property. Root: O.E. *circe* (church) and *wierde* (warden).

Cockarill see *Cockerell*.

Cockerell. In 1336 A.D. the Mayor of London decreed punishment by the whip for cockerels (poultry dealers) who failed to cleanse their poultry stalls at the close of a market day, or who defeathered their fowl in nearby public places. The Old French *cokerel* (cock trader) "second-named" today's *Cockerill*, *Cockarill*, *Cockrell*, and *Cockrill* in our phonebooks.

Cockerill see *Cockerell*.

Cockrell see *Cockerell*.

Cockrill see *Cockerell*.

Conner(s) identified the ancestor who was the official town ale tester and taster. If the ale was of poor quality, he declared its price to be set lower than market price. Root: O.E. *cunners* (inspector).

Day identified the ancestor who worked as a cheesemaker. Such a dairy worker in medieval times usually was a woman. By 1500 A.D. a DAY worker also referred to a person who worked on a day basis (usually an unskilled workman). Root: O.E. *daege* (dairy).

Deacon identified the ancestor who was a church assistant to a minister. Root: O.E. *deacon*.

Dean(e) identified an ancestor who was able to read and write. He often served as a keeper of records in a church or cathedral. In some churches he was employed as secretary to the minister. Root: O.E. *deen* (dean or official).

Gabler identified the ancestor who was a tax collector, and he was probably the most hated person in his community. Root: O. Fr. *gabellier* (tax collector).

Harder see *Herder*.

Hardrick see *Herder*.

Hardwick see *Herder*.

Herder. Sheep belonging to peasants in a village sometimes were collected by a herdsman who drove his small herd to a nearby common grazing green or meadow. These animals were gathered "as soon as the dew be gone", to be returned "before the sun

80

waned". The sheep herder's dog was trained to drive the animals "to and fro": high shrill notes of its herder screeched "Go Seek! Go Seek!," and low sustained tones commanded, "Come Home! Come Home!" Root: O. Dan. *hyrde* and O.E. *hyerdemann*. Variations include: *Harder, Hirdman, Hardwick* or *Hardrick* (cattle pasture).

Hirdman see *Herder*.

Jewell identified an ancestor who specialized in jewelry making. Such a craftsman usually was a "master" silversmith and goldsmith. In medieval days some of the best jewelry artisans were monastery monks who made gem ornaments for important abbots and bishops. Root: O. Fr. *jouel* (jewel).

Ketcher see *Catcher*.

Pound identified the ancestor who was the village or town "animal catcher". (Similar to today's dog-catcher.) An animal's owner had to prove the strayed animal was his property and he paid a small fine to regain the animal. Root: O.E. *pyndan* (to catch and hold).

Prior and *Pryor* identified the ancestor who was next in authority at a monastery. Root: O. Fr. *priour* (prior).

Pryor see *Prior*.

Sargent identified the ancestor who was in charge of a knight's armor and weapons. In early Norman-French times a "sergant" was a servant. Root: O. Fr. *sergant*.

Sexton identified the ancestor who was in charge of a church's religious equipment. Root: O.E. *secrestevn* (sacristan or sexton).

Sherwin identified the ancestor who served as a town messenger. He usually was a very fast runner. Root: O.E. *cyttan* (to cut) and *wind* ("to cut the wind" or "speed it up").

A *Squire* was a young man apprenticing for knighthood. He practiced mounting his horse with weights attached to his waist in order to strengthen his arm, leg, and hip muscles. Such practice was to get him ready to ride into battle in full body armor, burdened with sword, shield, and lance. The ceremony of knighthood required him to leap onto his horse, fully armed, and with no stirrup contact. Training for knighthood required seven or eight years of hard practice. Squires started training for knighthood at age eleven or twelve.

— — — — — — — — — —

Tilting at a quintain was a favorite pastime of young squires in the Middle Ages. The quintain was a stuffed dummy dressed as a knight. In worn-out armor it had a fixed shield in one hand and a club or sandbag in the other hand. The quintain was made to pivot in a complete circle. If the squire made a weak thrust from horseback at this dummy, it would spin round and swat the squire solidly with the club or sandbag.

— — — — — — — — — —

Swain identified the youthful ancestor who worked as a servant in a large house. Root: O. Nor. *sveinn* (young servant). By 1400 A.D. the words swain and swine evidently were used interchangeably so swain also referred to a herder of swine.

Vicker(s) identified the ancestor who was the assistant to a parish priest. *Vickers* usually identified the vicar's servant. Root: O.E. *viker*.

Waite(man) identified the ancestor who was the town night watchman. His duties were to be alert for fire, enemy attack, or to challenge a suspicious night stranger. Root: O.E. *wayte* (watchman).

- - - - - - - - - -

The CURSING WELL at St. Elian graveyard, located in North Wales, was a dreaded torture receptacle for the bewitching of victims - for a fee. A nearby sorceress could be hired to place a curse on one's enemy. The witch created a victim figure jabbed full of pins or wooden splinters, and this damned doll was then thrown into the "cursing well".

If the victim learned of this maledictive deed, she or he could pay another sorcerer to remove the victim's "figure" from the well's depths. St. Elian was a sixth century non-biblical Welsh saint.

- - - - - - - - - -

- OCCUPATION NAMES from MEDIEVAL SHOPKEEPERS -

The ten most common occupational family names in today's phone books identify at least six million persons in America:

Baker	Miller	Turner
Carter	Smith	Walker
Clark	Taylor	Wright
Hall		

Aleman identified the ancestor who made ale. Ale is a liquor fermented from the mixture of malt (barley), yeast, and water. It is darker, thicker, and more bitter than beer. Government officials in the Middle Ages regularly checked the alemaker's product to determine its quality. If it contained too much water, its price had to be reduced. Root: O.E. *alu*. See *Conner(s)*.

Bacon was a medieval occupational name for a pork butcher. "Bacon" was another name for pork. Root: O. Fr. *bacoun* (bacon).

Badger identified the ancestor who made small leather pouches and bags. Pocketbooks were unknown in the Middle Ages. Men and women wore a small leather pouch or sack tied to a belt or sash. Such a money bag was called a "purse". Root: O.E. *purs*. A street peddler who usually sold fish, butter, cheese, and eggs was often referred to as a "badger" since he carried his wares in a large bag or pouch.

Baker. This is one of the oldest occupational names. Root: O.E. *bacan* (to dry by heat or to bake). See *Baxter*.

Bannister identified the basketmaker ancestor. Baskets of all sizes were always in use in all medieval households. Root: O. Fr. *banastre* (basket). *Corbell* is a variation.

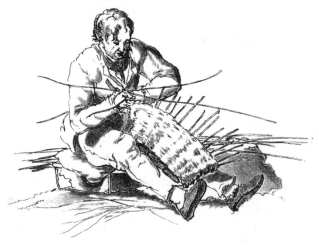

Barber see CASTLES and OCCUPATIONAL NAMES.

Barker identified the ancestor who tanned leather hides. Such a craftsman soaked raw animal skins in a solution of hot water and oak-bark which softened and "browned" the skin to be used for leather products. Root: O.E. *barkere* (barker).

Baxter identified a medieval female baker. *Baxter* was a later name-form for "bakester". See *Baker*.

Beaman (*Beeman*) identified the ancestor who raised bees. Honey was the only sweetening food available in the Middle Ages since modern sugar was not in use at that period of history. Sweets were made by mixing fruits, nuts, and honey. Root: O.E. *beo* (bee).

Beane identified the ancestor shopkeeper who grew and sold beans, a cheap basic food for poor people. Root: O.E. *bean*.

Blades identified the ancestor who made short knives, a very common tool and weapon carried by boys and men. Although knives were used to cut meat during a meal, it was rarely used to slice bread. They preferred to tear bread into pieces. Perhaps there may have been a medieval superstition about slicing bread? Root: O.E. *blaed*.

Boler, *Bowles* identified the ancestor who made bowls of wood, clay, or copper. Root: O.E. *bolla* (bowl).

Bolger (*Boulger*) identified the ancestor who made large leather bags used to store or carry objects. Saddle bags to fit a horse's flanks were his specialty. Root: O. Fr. *boulgier* (leather bag maker).

Boulger see *Bolger*.

Bowles see *Bolger*.

85

Brewer was an ale maker. See *Aleman.*

Brewster identified a female brewer. See *Aleman.*

Butcher identified the ancestor who slaughtered and sold fresh pork, beef, and mutton. Root: O. Fr. *bouchiere* (butcher).

Camber identified the ancestor who made combs from animal horn. Also known as *Comber, Comer,* and *Horner.* Root: O.E. *camb* (comb).

Capp and *Capper* identified the maker of head coverings. Root: O.E. *caeppa* (cap).

- - - - - - - - - -

> Why do we say A FEATHER IN HIS CAP? Men in medieval times enjoyed using feathers as ornamentation in the caps they usually wore. When a man was unusually brave or gallant, he was given a brightly-colored feather to stick in his cap.

- - - - - - - - - -

Chandler identified the ancestor who made candles. Most poor people went to bed soon after sunset. Candles were affordable only by the upper classes. Root: O. Fr. *candelier* (candle maker).

Cheeseman identified the ancestor who made cheese, a daily, common food for poor and rich. Medieval farmers used all of their milk to make cheese. Milk from sheep, goats, and cows could be varied in flavor by adding seeds or herbs. Peasants could work long hours, and warriors often marched and fought on a diet of cheese and hard bread. Early twelfth century French cheesemakers soon were bynamed *Ferma(n)ger, Firma(n)ger,* and *Furmager,* from the Old French *fromagier* (cheesemaker). After 1200 A.D. the Old English *cese* was extended into such bynames as: *Ches(e)man, Chisman, Ches-ler, Chesley, Chessman,* and *Cheswick* or *Chisholm* (places of cheese making). *Ewart, Yeoward,* and *Yeowart* identified medieval sheepherding ancestors who made soft and hard cheese exclusively from ewes' milk. Root: O.E. *eown* (ewe) and *hierde* (herder).

Ches(e)man see *Cheeseman.*

Chesler see *Cheeseman.*

Chesley see *Cheeseman.*

Chesman see *Cheeseman.*

Chessman see *Cheeseman.*

Cheswick see *Cheeseman.*

Chisholm see *Cheeseman.*

Chisman see *Cheeseman.*

Cockrell identified a seller of chickens, geese, and eggs. A roasted goose was a very popular medieval dish to serve on holidays, especially for Christmas. Some poultry men raised swans and peacocks to sell. These were roasted without removing the feathers. Root: O.E. *coccerel* (poultry). See *Hen-man.*

Comber see *Camber.*

Comer identified the ancestor who made and sold combs of seashell, animal horn, wood, or metal. Combs were in special demand by the ladies and were made only by order of a customer. Root: O.E. *camb* (comb). *Camber* is a variation name. See *Horner* and *Camber.*

Corbell see *Bannister.*

Crocker identified the ancestor who was a potter, specializing in the making of crocks. These clay jugs or pots were usually used to pickle meats, vegetables, or sometimes fruits. Most medieval townspeople had at least two crocks in use at all times. Root: O.E. *crocc* (clay pot). *Croker* was a variation spelling.

Croker see *Crocker*.

Culpepper see *Pepper(man)*.

Cuyler see *Collier*.

Diller (*Dillman*) identified the ancestor who grew and sold dill which was a cultivated plant in great demand in the Middle Ages. It was a carminative herb used to control gas in the stomach or bowels. The plant's spicy seeds and leaves were used for pickling foods. Root: O.E. *dile*.

Draper identified the ancestor who manufactured and sold textiles (chiefly of wool). Since much of his materials were sold overseas, a draper usually was a very wealthy trader. Root: O. Fr. *drapier* (draper or cloth maker).

Ewart see *Cheeseman*.

Fennell identified the ancestor who sold spices, often specializing in the fennel herb. The herb was used to add aroma to gravy or sauce in medieval cooking. Fennel leaves were dried and ground into a powder. In this form the spice retained its flavor for a long time. Root: O.E. *fenal* (fennel).

Ferma(n)ger see *Cheeseman*.

Firma(n)ger see *Cheeseman*.

Furmager see *Cheeseman*.

Golightly see *Messenger*.

Goodale identified the ancestor who made good ale. See *Aleman*.

Gravener see *Grosvenor* in CASTLES and OCCUPA-TIONAL NAMES.

Henman identified the ancestor who specialized in egg selling, preferring to breed hens chiefly for egg laying. Root: O.E. *henn*. See *Cockerell*.

Herring identified the ancestor who was a herring fisherman. Herring was always in great demand in the Middle Ages, chiefly for soup making. Root: O.E. *herring*.

Horner identified the ancestor who used animal horn to make spoons, scoops, mugs, drinking horns, lantern panes, inkwells, ornaments for horse harnesses, and uncomplicated musical wind instruments. Root: O.E. *horn*. See *Camber, Comer*.

Hood identified an ancestor who made hoods. In cold or rainy weather a head covering was necessary for poor and rich. Hoods of leather and cloth were also made to cover a falcon's (hawk's) head when the bird was not in pursuit of game birds. Knights always wore a special thick hood under their helmets. A hood always covered the neck as well as the head. Root: O.E. *hod* (hood).

- - - - - - - - - -

Why do we say FALSEHOOD? During the Middle Ages the wearing of a hood frequently indicated what kind of work a man did. Tradesmen, professional men, and religious officers wore hoods of different shapes and colors. A dishonest person could pretend to be a doctor by wearing a doctor's hood. He also could be arrested and jailed "for wearing a false hood." Over the centuries this medieval idea of deception became today's FALSEHOOD (a lie or distortion of fact).

- - - - - - - - - -

Inman identified the ancestor who was an innkeeper. An inn or tavern was the medieval roadside motel. Inns (taverns) served food and ale. One room might be set aside for gambling games. Horsebacked guests paid extra for their animal. Guests often slept two or three in a bed, each a stranger to the other. An uncomfortable mattress was filled with chicken or goose feathers and usually was full of vermin. Sometimes a guest was made drunk by the innkeeper and then robbed in the middle of the night. Such was the reputation of inns or taverns outside and beyond the walls of a town. Taverns within a town were very respectable and honorable. *Taverner* and *Osler* are other occupational names for *Inman*.

Massinger see *Messenger*.

A Middle Ages *Messenger* was considered to be the prince of travelers on the king's highways: he had to be a good horseman, able to survive all hazards of weather, experienced at avoiding conflict on the road or in an inn, and quick-witted enough to suspect a conspiracy to steal his message-pouch. Today's family names of *Messenger*, *Massinger*, *Trotter*, *Golightly* and *Sherwin* came from medieval ancestors who served as messengers on foot or on horseback.

Osler see *Inman*.

Patton identified the ancestor who made clog shoes. These were sandal-type footwear made from wood with a high heel and leather straps. "Pattons" probably were designed in a monastery, for they were first worn by monks. Clog sandals enabled one's feet to keep dry when walking in mud or on wet ground. Root: O.Fr. *patene* (clog shoe).

Peck identified the ancestor who made quarter-bushel-sized baskets which were in much demand by the medieval housewife. They were used to store food products. Root: O.E. *pek* (peck).

Pepper(man) identified the ancestor who sold pepper. This spice was in great demand during the Middle Ages. Lack of refrigeration spoiled meat quickly. It was medieval practice to use pepper to conceal the stale taste of spoiled meat.

Plummer identified the ancestor who sold feathers. Goose and chicken feathers were used to make large bed pillows and mattresses. Down feathers from ducks were useful to stuff bedding for the cold weather. Men and women liked to wear a feather in their caps and hats. Peacock feathers were used as wall and furniture decorations. Also spelled *Plumer*. Root: O.Fr. *plume* (feather).

Pottiker identified the ancestor who sold medicines (today's druggist or pharmacist). A pottiker (apothecary) was permitted to prescribe salves and medicines: a dried, chopped-up toad's liver for dizziness or liver ailment; goose fat to be used as a salve for pimples; urine from a male dog or goat to be applied to severe skin itching. Root: O. Fr. *apotecaire* (apothecary).

Potts and *Potter* identified the ancestor who made dishes, bowls, and mugs for preparing or storing food and for drinking. The potter's products of clay were in great demand as medieval towns and cities developed. In most thirteenth century homes a family ate from a single large bowl, each person using the same crude wooden spoon. Bread was used to soak up any liquid in the family bowl. Meat was eaten with the fingers. Root: O.E. *pottere* (potter).

Prentice and *Prentiss* identified the ancestor who was an apprentice (learning a trade). Root: O. E. *prentis* (apprentice).

Quarrie(y) identified the ancestor who worked in a quarry: an open pit or mine where stone was plentiful. A medieval quarry miner worked with a large hammer and wedges to remove usable stone from a pit. Stones were hauled on long, sturdy wooden sleds pulled by a team of oxen. Stone was needed for walls of fortresses, palaces, castles, and cathedrals. It also sold for use as grave markers and tombstones. Small stones were polished to pave courtyards or streets. By the thirteenth century many large buildings (including manor homes) were built with stone, greatly reducing the fire hazard of wood. Root: O. Fr. *quarreour* (quarry miner).

Reeder identified the ancestor who thatched roofs with reeds (tall grasses that grew in wetland places). Medieval roofs of reed or straw were a fire menace since a fire spread easily to other roofs in the town. Very rich persons used slate for roofing on their houses. *Thatcher* is another name for a *Reeder*. Root: O.E. *hreod* (reed).

Roper identified the ancestor who made and sold rope. It was an important article for sailing ships. Rope-making is an ancient craft that came to Europe and Britain from the Mediterranean region. Root: O.E. *rap* (rope).

Sadler identified the ancestor who made and sold saddles. The *Sadler* was a highly skilled craftsman. It took at least ten years for an apprentice to learn this trade. Root: O.E. *sadol* (saddle).

- - - - - - - - - -

> Royalty and noblemen required at least two saddles. One saddle was for tournament combat or battlefield action while the other saddle was used for hunting and traveling. The combat saddle had a saddletree or back (like a chair) to support the rider if he suffered a sudden, powerful lance blow. Women preferred a special saddle on which they sat facing sideways instead of facing forward.

- - - - - - - - - -

Saltman identified the ancestor who sold salt. Medieval food was preserved by drying, smoking, or salting. Most preservation of meat was done by salting (a pickling process). Salt was unrefined in the Middle Ages, and it therefore was full of harmful impurities. Root: O.E. *sealt*.

Sherwin see *Messenger*.

Slaughter identified the ancestor who bought live, domestic animals, butchered them, and sold pork, beef, and mutton from his butcher shop. Root: O.E. *slaughtere* (slaughterer).

Spicer identified the ancestor shopkeeper who sold herbs and spices for flavoring foods. Because of no refrigeration in medieval times, food often quickly spoiled in warm weather. Highly flavored and seasoned sauces and relishes were used to conceal the spoiled taste of such food. Much ginger, mustard, garlic, cinnamon, and pepper were used in these medieval sauces. Root: O. Fr. *espice* (spice).

Taverner see *Inman*.

Thatcher see *Reeder.*

Trotter see *Messenger.*

Yeoward see *Cheeseman.*

Yeowart see *Cheeseman.*

- OCCUPATION NAMES from TRADESMEN and CRAFTSMEN -

Medieval teenage boys usually learned the trade of their fathers. Some sought training away from home with a "master" tradesman.

The master tradesman usually hired a boy (at least age twelve) to serve as a helper or apprentice. This craftsman had to provide the boy with a bed, meals, some clothing, and a small salary. The length of apprenticeship was at least seven years. Every craftsman hoped that the apprentice's work would repay the master after two or three years.

At the end of six or seven years the apprentice could be declared a "journeyman." In eight or ten years he could apply to a guild or order to become rated as a "master" workman.

To become a "master" worker one had to join a craft guild (association or union). The workman submitted a sample of his skill. If it was judged of good quality, the tradesman was declared a "master" and accepted into the guild.

Obsolete occupational names from the thirteenth and fourteenth centuries include:

Shakelock - jailor
Slaymaker - shuttle maker
Massacrier - butcher
Flutter - flutist

Coifer - capmaker
Killebole - butcher
Disshere - dish maker
Wonter - mole catcher

94

Arrowsmith identified the ancestor who made steel arrowheads. Root: O.E. *arwe* (arrow) and *smitan* (to smite or strike).

Barrett identified the ancestor who made berets and caps. Today's beret came to England with the Norman-French in 1066 A.D. This style of headgear had no peak or brim and it had a snug-fitting headband. Made from wool, it was a head cover for every kind of weather. Root: O.E. *barrett* (beret).

Bellows identified the ancestor who worked in the blacksmith trade. A large leather air bag was pressed to blast more air into a smith's open furnace in order to create high heat for the shaping of metal. A *Bellows* usually was an apprentice who kept such a fire at its hottest temperature. Root: O.E. *belg* (blast bag).

Belt(er) identified the ancestor who made leather belts, a necessary part of a medieval costume for all ancestors except poor ones (who made their own crude belts from twisted plant fibers). Military men required a special belt to which they attached one or more small weapons. An archer needed a special belt to carry his pouch of arrows on his back. Most women and men needed a belt to which they attached a small pouch to carry keys, money, or a small prayer book. Pockets as we know them today were not invented until the sixteenth century. Root: O.E. *beltere* (belt maker).

Binder identified the ancestor who made books, printing the letters by hand. The binder made his own ink and brushes to print on lambskin, calfskin or kidskin. Such thin sheets of skin were secured by waxed cord and made into a book with covers of leather. With proper care these hand made books lasted for several hundred years. Root: O.E. *bindere* (binder).

Bissell see *Bushell*.

Boardman is from the Old English *bord* meaning board. See *Sawyer*.

Bolger identified the ancestor who was a leather craftsman. He made bags, sacks, and pouches. Medieval clothing had no pockets (which were not invented until the sixteenth century).

Booker see *Scribner*, *Clarke*.

Brashear identified an ancestor who worked in the brass trade. Brass workers made various hardware items that were often exposed to the outdoors: locks and keys for gates, doors, and coaches; also chest hinges and special fittings for horse harnesses. Small and large church memorial tablets usually were hammered from brass plating. Root: O.E. *brasian* (brass worker).

Bushell identified the ancestor who was a bushel craftsman. Bushel baskets were very useful for storing food indoors or outdoors, and they were in great demand in the Middle Ages. A medieval bushel equaled four pecks, and they had to pass official inspection to prove the bushels were of accurate measure. Root: O. Fr. *hoisselier* (bushel maker). *Bissell* was a later variation name.

Caird was an Irish occupational name for a metal worker. See *Smith*. Root: Irish *ceard* (metal craftsman).

Carpenter identified the ancestor who was a wood craftsman in the building industry. A carpenter usually did the rough framework for a cottage, home, or building. A "joiner" was a master carpenter who did the special finishing of a house or building. Root: O. Fr. *carpentier*. See *Cartwright*, *Wheelwright*, *Wheeler*.

Cartwright identified the ancestor who specialized in making two-wheel carts (a small wagon with oversized wheels). Carts in towns and villages were horse-drawn; and oxen hauled carts in the countryside. Root: O.E. *craet* (cart) and *wyrtha* (wright or carpenter).

Carver identified the ancestor who carved art objects from wood. Medieval churches and cathedrals were the carver's best customers; they ordered wooden pictures with scenes from Bible stories and of famous saints. *Carvers* also made wooden grave markers. Root: O.E. *ceorfan* (to carve).

Clarke identified the ancestor who could read and write. He served as a keeper of records and letter writer in a church, palace, or manor. Root: O.E. *clerke* (clerk). The name was pronounced as *Clark*. See *Scribner*. There are approximately 500,000 persons named *Clarke* in the U.S.A.

- A matter of CHAUCER'S GHOST
and a PHONEBOOK -

If Chaucer's ghost chose to thumb through a Los Angeles phonebook, he could be astounded to see several hundred *Clark(e)s* listed therein. The Ghost might decide to insert among these *Clark(e)* columns the following note:

"Be it told that til before 1200 A.D. most persons in the land did speke French in many castles and in all apartements of kings whilst in many vallees som Anglo-Saxons never forget their auncien tunge. In towns the comun folks did speke Inglish...

"Be it told that le clerc (*Clark*), who learnt his Latin, was needed for all legal documents and these were wrytten down in Latin. the Norman French in 1088 A.D. speked him as le latinier (the *Latiner*), whilst the *Inglish* by 1200 A.D. writt him as *Lattimore*. Betwixt these years le clerc (*Clark*), was y-cleped *Latner* and *Lattimore* -- according to eche maner of speking in each shyer of Yngeland.

"Be it told forsooth after 1200 A.D. that any ancestre who could rede and write was y-cleped *Clark* and he was esely wayting in the market place -- always ready to write, for woerth of coyne, a delikat note of love, a lettre of complaynt, or a papyre of bisiness for a marchant.

"At his belt hung a small lethre pouche of inke-poudre. In his peakt cap was a gose quill, at once reddy for use. He was a man
'Than can no more what he shall wryte
But as his maister besyde dothe endyte.'"

- - - - - - - - - -

Our use of "x" for a kiss at the closing of a letter originated in the Middle Ages when it was the custom to sign a legal document with the symbol of the cross of St. Andrew. (This saint's sword-symbol resembles an "x".) The signer had to kiss his mark of a cross to pledge his commitment to the official affidavit. This legal pledging custom was no longer in use by 1700 A.D. yet lovers continued the use of this "kiss of good faith (x)" in their intimate messages and letters.

- - - - - - - - - -

Coleman identified the ancestor who made charcoal. This was an important fuel for various metal workers to burn in their furnaces. "Charcoal" was the medieval word for "coal". Wood was burned to make charcoal. Coke, however, is made from coal, and is a modern process of production. Variations include: *Collier*, *Collyer,* and *Cuyler*. Root: O.E. *col* (coal).

Collier and *Collyer* see *Coleman*.

Cooper(man) identified the ancestor who made small and large tubs and barrels which were in great demand in medieval times, especially for transporting wine or grain overseas. Root: O. Fr. *couper* (cooper). *Cowper* was a later spelling for *Cooper*. *Tubman* and *Tubbs* were other names for a *Cooper*. Root: O.E. *couper* (barrel maker).

Corbell is from the Old French *corbellier* meaning basket maker. See *Bannister* and *Bushell*.

Corden and *Cordin* identified the ancestor who was a shoemaker. The finest leather for shoes came from Cordova, Spain. *Corden* and *Cordin* as occupational names identified "one who worked with Cordovan leather." Root: O. Fr. *cordoanier* (leather worker). *Cordiner* and *Corwin* are variation names.

Cordin see *Corden*.

Cordiner see *Corden*.

Corwin see *Corden*.

Couchman identified the ancestor who was an upholsterer and a maker of couches. Only royalty, nobility, or upper class persons could afford to be customers to a couchmaker. Thereby a medieval couchmaker often became a member of the wealthy class. Root: O. Fr. *coucheur* (couchmaker).

Cowler identified the ancestor who made hooded garments for friars, pilgrims, and monks. Such a garment usually was made of rough, woolen cloth. A belt of rope was worn to gather the garment's loose folds. This rope belt was a symbolic reminder of the anguish of Christ as he was led to the spot of crucifixion. Root: O.E. *cugele* (cowl or hood).

Cowper see *Cooper(man)*.

Custer identified the ancestor who made cushions and bed pads filled with feathers. Peasants customarily slept on an earth floor, using a pad filled with straw or grass as a mattress. Upper-class persons slept in a bed on a feather-stuffed mattress. In monasteries monks slept in their day clothing on a coarse woolen sheet. Only wealthy persons could afford to have fancy cushions made. Root: O. Fr. *coustier*.

Cutler identified the ancestor who made various shapes of knives. Medieval women, because they were often in danger of violent attack from a stranger if they ventured alone in an isolated place,

100

frequently carried small daggers.   Root: O. Fr.
cotelier (cutler).

Daber.   Returning warriors from the Crusades introduced plastered walls into Britain; by 1300 A.D. it
was a popular English middle-ages feature in house
construction,   referred   to   as   "daub   and   wattle"
(plaster onto matted stakes).   Its medieval usage is
evidenced from the several bynames for men who
labored at this new construction process: *Da(u)ber*,
Dawber, *Dober(ed)*, and *Daberman* or *Doberman*.
Root: from O. Fr. *daubier* (plasterer).

Dawber see *Daber.*

Dober(ed) see *Daber.*

Doberman see *Daber.*

Farris see *Farrar.*

Farrar identified an ancestor who shoed horses.   It
was a Norman-French name for a blacksmith.   Root:
O. Fr. *ferrier* (blacksmith).

Ferrer see *Farrar.*

Ferris see *Farrar.*

Fisher   and   *Fisk*   identified   a   fisherman   ancestor.
Root: O.E. *fiscere* (fisherman).   A small chopped
fish cooked as a soup, served with much bread, often   was   a   complete   evening   meal   for   a   poor,
medieval family.

Fryer   identified   the   ancestor   who   was   a   friar,
serving as a priest although he was not so ordained.
He   usually   worked   as   a   missionary   among   poor
people,   appearing   at   markets,   fairs,   and   festivals
where he preached about the evils of sin.   A friar
supported   himself   by   begging.   Root: O. Fr. *frer*
(brother).

101

Glass(man) identified the ancestor who was a craftsman for glass products. The master tradesman who made stained glass for church and cathedral display was always highly esteemed because of his artistic skill. Root: O.E. *glaes* (glass).

Glover identified the glove-making ancestor. The fine art of glovemaking was brought to medieval English by Flemish immigrants. Gloves were made of leather or cloth and were in great demand. Hunters needed thick gloves to protect their wrists from falcon claws. The hunter usually walked about with his falcon (hawk) perched on his wrist. To offer a glove to a person was a special sign of friendship. Root: O.E. *glof* (glove).

Goff and *Gough* are Welsh names for *Smith*. Root: Welsh *gowff* (to hammer metal). See *Smith*.

Goldsmith identified the ancestor who was a master craftsman with gold. All his jewelry usually consisted of special orders of gold styling for royalty, nobility, or wealthy churchmen. Root: O.E. *gold*.

Gove see *Goff*.

Gow see *Goff*.

Hooper is a variation of *Cooper*. Root: O.E. *hopere*.

Joiner identified the ancestor who was a master carpenter. After a carpenter built the rough structure of a house or building, the joiner finished it with special wood paneling, ornamentation, and other fittings. Root: O. Fr. *joignour* (joiner or wood finisher).

Keeler identified an ancestor who was skilled at making keels for ships. Root: O.E. *cellod* (keel).

Ledbetter identified the ancestor who was a craftsman with lead. Cathedral and palace roofs were made from lead sheets which a worker hammered into smooth perfection before these were attached to a roof. In the eastern part of England such a lead tradesman was named *Plummer* Roots: O.E. *lead* (lead worker) and O. Fr. *plombier* (lead worker).

Lorimer identified the ancestor who made spurs, stirrups, and bridles for horses. Root: O. Fr. *loremiere* (maker of spurs).

Nedler identified the ancestor who made and sold needles of many sizes for many uses. By 1300 A.D. needles were as common a household necessity as were kitchen knives. The sewing of leather, wool, or cotton products were always done by hand since sewing machines were unknown in the Middle Ages. Root: O.E. *noedl* (needle).

Naylor identified the ancestor who made and sold nails of several sizes. Very often he was asked to make nails, bolts, or spikes for large castle gates, for massive, heavy doors in a cathedral, or for horse-drawn coaches. A "naylor" was a specialized smith who had to know how to shape metal for use as nails. He was sometimes referred to as *Naysmith*. Root: O.E. *noegel* (nail).

Netter identified the ancestor who was a skillful maker of nets which he needed to catch fish or birds. The fish when caught had to be sold at market by the following day or they spoiled. Captured birds were kept in cages and sold alive in the town market. Fish and birds were much lower in price than meat. Root: O.E. *netere* (netter).

Pittman and *Pitts* trade named the ancestor who worked in a pit as a clay digger.

Plummer see *Ledbetter*.

Sawyer - The construction of a medieval building was a cumbersome and lengthy process. Oxen or horses hauled logs to the building site where timbers were prepared by the use of crude saws and wedges. A large tree was reduced to needed board sizes after several days of trimming and sawing. The occupational "byname" for the carpenter was *Sawyer* which later varied as *Sayer(s)*, *Sears*, and *Seyers*. Root: O. Dan. *zaag* and O.E. *saga* (saw). *Boardman* is a variation for *Sawyer*.

Sayer(s) see *Sawyer*.

Saylor   Identified the ancestor who worked as a seaman. To work aboard a ship was a great attraction for a medieval young man who wanted adventure and excitement. It also was a risky and dangerous kind of work. Root: O.E. *segl* (to sail).

Scribner   identified the ancestor who copied manuscripts and books in a cathedral. Root: O. Fr. *excrivain* (scrivenor or copier). *Booker* was a later variation for *Scribner*. See *Clarke*.

Seaman is from the Old English *sae* (the sea). See *Saylor*.

Sears see *Sawyer*.

Shinner see *Skinner*.

Shipman is from the Old English *scip-mann* meaning "shipman". See *Saylor*.

Shoemaker   identified the ancestor who made and sold shoes. Root: O.E. *scoh* (shoe). Shoes were never ready-made in the Middle Ages. The customer came to the shoemaker's shop to order made-to-measure shoes.

Skinner identified the ancestor who was skillful as a skinner of animal hides. Root: O.E. *scinn* (skin) *Shinner* was a variation.

Slater identified the ancestor who used slate for roofing. Only nobleman or wealthy merchants could afford a slate roof; poor people used mud and straw. Root: O.E. *sclate* (slate).

- Those many SMITHS
in our PHONE BOOKS -

The long lists of *Smith* names in our phone books are a reminder of the many metalworkers who worked at this trade in the Middle Ages. The local smith was the man of skill and inventiveness with any kind of metal used in products for farming, building construction, jewelry making, or battle action.

A *Smith* was always highly respected and honored for his skill with metals. Such men were very specialized "mechanics" with exact occupational names to identify their specialties. Such a wide variety probably accounts for the fact that *Smith* is the most frequent family name in America and in Britain. Root: O.E. *smitan* (to smite or stike with a hammer). See *Farrar, Goff*.

Armsmith	Locksmith
Arrowsmith	Minsmith (coin minter)
Axsmith	Nailsmith
Bellsmith	Platesmith
Bowsmith	Plowsmith
Bucklesmith	Potsmith (metal pots)
Coopersmith (metal tubs)	Ringsmith (armor chains)
Coppersmith	Scythesmith
Goldsmith	Shoesmith (horse shoes)
Greensmith (lead)	Silversmith
Gunsmith	Spearsmith
Hammersmith	Swordsmith
Knifesmith	

Preparation for battle action was an important castle routine during the Middle Ages. Each nobleman maintained his own small army of knights, archers, spearmen, and battle weapons. In 1181 A.D.

English King Henry II required that every freeman in the land must own a battle helmet, shield, and spear as preparation for future battle duty.

From 1100 A.D. to 1300 A.D. a metalworker's occupational name usually was spelled *Smith* or *Smithe*. From 1300 A.D. to 1600 A.D. this spelling changed to *Smyth* and *Smythe*. By 1700 A.D. it was generally spelled as *Smith* again.

By 1450 A.D. *Smith* had become an inherited name. John Smith, the first *Smith* to come to America, arrived here in 1630 as a military leader rather than as a metal worker.

There are more than two million Americans named Smith, according to Elsdon C. Smith, author of <u>The Book of Smith</u>.

Below is a a list of John Smiths in other countries:

Arabia	Yahya Kaddah
Belgium	Jehan De Smet
Bulgaria	Ivan Kovac
Czechoslovakia	Jan Kovar
Denmark	Johan Smed
Finland	Jussi Seppanen
France	Jean Lefevre
Germany	Johann Schmidt
Greece	Ioannes Skmiton
Holland	Jan Smid
Hungary	Janos Kovacs
Ireland	Sean Gough, Goff
Italy	Giovanni Feffaro
Lapland	Jofan Smirjo
Mexico	Juan Herrara
Norway	Johannes Smid
Poland	Jan Kowal
Portugal	Hoao Ferreiro
Russia	Ivan Kuznetzov
Scotland	Ian Gow
Spain	Juan Herrera
Sweden	Johan Smed

Turkey	Iabaja Temirzi
Wales	Evan Goff, Gowan

Smithe see *Smith.*

Smyth(e) see *Smith.*

Steele identified the ancestor who was a craftsman with steel, a metal which was used chiefly for weapons (especially swords) in the Middle Ages. Root: A.S. *stele.*

Stone(man) is from the Old English *stan* (stone) and *mann* (man). See *Mason* in CASTLES and OCCUPATIONAL NAMES, and *Quarrie(y)* in OCCUPATIONAL NAMES from MEDIEVAL SHOPKEEPERS.

Taylor identified the ancestor who made men's tunics, capes, shirts, hosiery, and other coverings for the legs. Royalty and nobility usually had one or more tailors in their employ. Root: O. Fr. *tailleor* (tailor).

Tanner identified the ancestor who prepared animal pelts to sell to leather craftsmen. A *Tanner* used whale oil or animal fat to make rawhide smooth. Root: O.E. *tannere* (tanner). *Barker* was another name for a tanner. See *Barker.*

Thatcher identified the ancestor who repaired or made roofs from grasses or reeds. Root: O.E. *theccanere* (thatcher). *Reeder* also identified a roofer. See *Reeder.*

Tinker identified the ancestor who was a metalworker. He specialized in making pewter bowls, dishes, and mugs. Pewter was made from a small amount of copper and a large amount of tin. Medieval middle class families could not afford gold or silver tableware, but they felt very stylish when they could afford pewter table objects. In Ireland a tinker was a kind of vagabond repairer of pots and pans; he traveled from town to town in a wagon,

107

shaking a "plinking, tinkling" bell to announce that he was in the village. Root: O.E. *tinkere*.

Toler and *Toller* identified the ancestor who worked as a toll collector at a bridge, road, or woods. Medieval lords usually required merchants or other travelers to pay a toll (tax) to pass through a village, highway, woods, or over a bridge of a stream. Collecting a toll at such places was customary in the Middle Ages. *Towle(r)*, *Tollman*, and *Tolman* were variations. Root: O.E. *tollere* (toll collector). See *Travis*.

Tol(l)man see *Toler*.

Towle(r) see *Toler*.

Trapp(e) identified the ancestor who hunted game by using only traps and snares. Root: O.E. *traeppe*.

Traves see *Travis*.

Travis identified the ancestor who collected tolls at a river crossing, at a city gate, or at at bridge. Root: O. Fr. *travers* (to pass over or cross over). *Travis* is the modern form of *Traves*. See *Toler*.

Tubbs identified the ancestor who made wooden tubs rather than barrels. See *Cooper(man)*.

Tubman see *Cooper(man)*.

Turner identified an ancestor who made round objects of wood by the use of a lather. He "turned" special wood pieces that were fastened on his lather (a wood-turning machine) to create a bowl, mug, or similar article. Root: O. Fr. *tournour* (turner).

Tyler identified the ancestor who made tile floors for palaces, manor halls, cathedrals, and churches. A medieval tiler was often honored for his skill with tiles.

Wainwright identified the ancestor who made wagons. Merchants needed wagons to transport their merchandise over short distances. The medieval wagon had no springs. Moving over dirt highways full of holes and ruts, wagons suffered loosening joints and other wear, and required constant repair. Root: A.S. *waegnwyrhta* (wagon maker).

Wheeler identified the ancestor who made wheels. Early Middle Ages cart wheels had no spokes, being made of solid boards nailed together and then sawed off to make a usable wheel. However, spoked wheels came into use soon after 1200 A.D. Root: O.E. *hweol* (wheel).

Whittier identified the leather craftsman who specialized in prepared white leather for gloves and footwear. Root: O.E. *hwitan* (to whiten). *Whytere* and *Wyter* were medieval spellings.

- OCCUPATION NAMES
from the COUNTRYSIDE -

During the Middle Ages about ninety percent of the population lived and worked on large plantations

109

(manors). A manor nobleman gave protection to peasants by offering them work in a fortified settlement. Strong, high walls around the manor village protected peasants from savage animals. The nobleman's army of soldiers prevented attacks from roving clans of strangers.

Peasants (serfs) lived in crude shelters or huts which were not weather tight. Such shelters were made of crossed saplings stuffed with grass and mud; and these huts had no chimneys or windows. Fireplace smoke escaped through a small hole in the roof.

Most peasants in a medieval settlement kept a hand-made spearhead which they fixed easily to the handle of a hoe as a defense against robbers. A blast from the hayward's horn was a warning that an outlaw or fugitive was in the village. The peasants used their temporary spears to pursue the villain in their midst.

A peasant's death was an event that required payment of a *heriot* (feudal tax) to his landlord and church. If the peasant owned two cattle, his lord had first heriot choice, and the bishop had second choice. In the towns the same feudal law of *heriot* allowed the church choice of a piece of warm clothing, a brass kettle, or even the large bed in which the person had died.

Ackerman identified an ancestor who was a field worker or farmer. *Acker(s)* and *Akers* are variations. The manor plantation cultivated all its necessary food. The "villeins" or peasant workers paid for the use of their land in farm products, military service, and sometimes in small amounts of money. Root: O.E. *acer* (acre) and *mann* (man) or "acreman."

Acker(s) see *Ackerman*.

Akers see *Ackerman*.

Daily foods in the Middle Ages were
bread, cheese, peas, beans, poultry,
and meat when available. Commonfolk
raised pigs which were never as fat
as today's pigs. Since much of the
pig was preserved for winter use, salt
was in great demand to preserve this
meat for long periods of time. Middle
Ages ancestors ate only two meals
daily.

Beaman   identified the ancestor who specialized in
producing honey. Cakes and other sweets used only
honey since sugar was not yet in common use in
England.   Also spelled *Beeman*.   Root: O.E. *beo*
(bee) and *mann*(man).

Beeman see *Beaman*.

Bond   identified the ancestor who was not a
freeman to work wherever he pleased. He was "in
bond" or "bound" to the nobleman's plantation. He
sometimes owned the house in which he lived. Root:
O.E. *bonda* (bound).

Bridgor see *Bridgman*.

Bridges see *Bridgman.*

Brigham see *Bridgman.*

Bridgman. In 1148 A.D. King Henry II, grandson of William the Conqueror, decreed that the repairing of bridges on the king's highway was the responsibility of the nobleman whose estate bordered this Royal roadway. The king's unpopular edict was sweetened with the proviso that allowed the lord to collect a toll from all wayfarers and merchants who crossed such a bridge. Variations of *Bridgman* (toll collector) include: *Bridger*, *Bridges* (bridge workman); *Bridgen*, *Briggins* (lived at the end of the bridge); *Brigham* (lived and worked near the bridge); *Briggs* (toll collector); and *Brigsley* (lived in the meadow near the bridge). Bridge is rooted in the Old English *brvcg.*

Bullard identified the ancestor who was a herder of bulls. Root: O.E. *bula* (bull) and *hierde* (herder).

Bundy is a variation of *Bond*. See *Bond.*

Calvert identified the ancestor who tended and herded calves. Root: O.E. *calf* (calf) and *hierde* (herder).

Coker identified an ancestor who worked as a hayman: cutting and reaping hay and stacking the hay into a pile (hay cock). Root: O.E. *cokke* (cone-shaped stack of hay).

Colt identified an ancestor who tended colts, usually in an enclosure. Root: O.E. *colt*. *Coltard* (herder), *Coltman*, and *Coultard* (herder) are variations.

Coltard see *Colt.*

Coltman see *Colt.*

112

Coultard see *Colt*.

Coward   identified an ancestor who herded cows.
Root: O.E. *cuhyrde* (cow herder).

- - - - - - - - - -

Why do we say DAUGHTER? Years
and years before the Middle Ages it
was   the   custom   of   Anglo-Saxon
families in Britain to have a daughter
milk the family cow.   The Anglo-
Saxon word for a milkmaid was *doh-*
tor, the root of today's DAUGHTER.

- - - - - - - - - -

Deeker see *Dickman*.

Deeks see *Dickman*.

Deetcher see *Dickman*.

Deykes see *Dickman*.

Dickerman see *Dickman*.

Dickers see *Dickman*.

Dickman.   Low-lying farmland near rapid streams often required the digging of dikes or ditches to contain or redirect the river overflow. It was also the custom of bird hunters to enlarge a wetland strip by digging ditches through a stream bank to attract more birds to this wetland site.   Such birds were captured alive by the use of special nets.   Today's phonebook names of *Deeker*, *Deeks*, *Deetcher*, *Deykes*, *Dykes*, *Dickers*, and *Dickerman* are byname extensions of dike and ditch. Root: O.E. *dic* (dike or ditch).

Driver   identified an ancestor who herded cattle over long distances, usually to be sold at a market. Root: O.E. *drivere*.

Dykes see *Dickman*.

Farmer   identified the ancestor who operated a farm. Root: O. Fr. *fermier*.

Fincher   identified the ancestor who trapped finch birds, considered a delicacy in the Middle Ages. Root: O.E. *finc*.

Fisher   identified the ancestor who was a fisherman. Root: O.E. *fisc* (fish).

Forrest(er)   identified the ancestor who was a forest guardian for a king or nobleman. His chief

114

duty was to keep away poachers or robbers who sought to hide in a dense forest (which was too large to be fenced). Root: O.E. *forest*. *Foster* is a variation for *Forrester*. See *Parker*.

Foster see *Forrester*.

Forward identified the ancestor who was a swineherder. Root: O.E. *for* (pig) and *weard* (herder or warden).

Freeman identified the ancestor who could own land. He was not a serf (slave) on a plantation. Root: O.E. *fremann* (the free man).

- - - - - - - - - -

The Norman-French brought the word *villein* to England in 1066 A.D. It was the medieval French nickname for a serf, peasant, or any poor person. Over the centuries the spelling and meaning of *villein* changed into today's villain which means "the bad guy" or the lawbreaker.

- - - - - - - - - -

Gaither(s) identified the ancestor who tended goats. Root: O.E. *gat* (goat).

Gossard see *Goss(e)*.

Goss(e). Breeding geese in the Middle Ages was a special industry. Today there are at least fifteen family names that centuries ago were mere "bynames" for persons who bred and sold geese, or who lived near geese pens. Goose feathers were preferred by archers who wished to prevent their arrows from wobbling in transit. Goose down was valued for stuffing pillows and beddings. A special type of goose quill was used by most clerks. Today's variations include: *Gosford, Gosland, Goslin,*

Gosfield, *Gossard*, *Gossertt*, *Gozzett*, and *Joss(e)*. Root: from O. E. *gos*.

Gossertt see *Goss(e)*.

Gosfield identified a goose-breeding place. See *Goss(e)*.

Gosford identified a goose-breeding place. See *Goss(e)*.

Gosland identified a goose-breeding place. See *Goss(e)*.

Goslin see *Goss(e)*.

Gothard was another occupational name for a goatherder. Root: O.E. *gat* (goat) and *hierde* (herder).

Gozzett see *Goss(e)*.

Hacker identified the ancestor who was a woodcutter in a woods. He daily provided firewood for a castle or manor hall. Root: O.E. *hacce* (chop).

Haire identified a hare trapper or a person who lived near the shop sign of a hare. See *Hare*.

Harder identified the ancestor who herded sheep or cattle. Root: O.E. *heard* (herd).

116

Hare. As soon as a serf's child was able to move about without losing balance, it became a productive laborer: the child gathered nuts, berries, or fruits as well as tufts of wool which the sheep shed on bushes or on the ground, and feathers from wild birds abundant in the nearby forest. By age nine or ten such youngsters were considered mature laborers and were often required to set snares in the cleared fields or woods to trap wild hares. The lord of the estate claimed most or all of the pelts, occasionally permitting the snarer to keep one or two carcasses and pelts. The "bynames" from *Hare* have become: *Haire, Harfield, Harley, Hargrave(s), Hargreaves,* and *Hargrove.* Root: Dan. *hare* to O.E. *hara.*

Hargrave(s) see *Hare.*

Hargreave(s) see *Hare.*

Hargrove identified the person who lived and worked near a hare grove. See *Hare.*

Harley ideintified the person who lived near a field of hare burrows. See *Hare.*

Hayward see *Howard* in CASTLES and OCCUPATIONAL NAMES.

Hayes identified the ancestor who repaired fences or hedges (to keep animals from straying). Root:: O.E. *haw* (enclosed place).

Hefferan identified an ancestor who tended heifers (a cow not 3 years old which has not produced a calf). Root: O.E. *heafre* (heifer) and *mann* (man).

117

Hyde identified an ancestor who owned a piece of land of at least 60 acres called a "hide," an acreage that could be cultivated by a plow in one year. Root: *hid* (a section of land). *Hide* was a Middle Ages spelling.

Joss(e) see *Goss(e)*.

Lockhart identified the ancestor who attended sheep or cattle in an enclosed space. Root: O.E. *loc* (pen or corral) and *hierde* (herder, keeper).

Miller see CASTLES and OCCUPATIONAL NAMES.

- - - - - - - - - -

Nutrition Surname Fossils

Some family names in our phonebooks inform us of food items that were a part of the daily diet of medieval ancestors. Such surnames describe where such individuals lived and worked. *Barham* and *Barton* indentified barley sites. *Benfield* identified a bean field. *Dilworth* identified a dill field. *Otley* identified an oat field. *Riddell* and *Ryel* identified rye sites. *Whitfield* identified a wheat field.

- - - - - - - - - -

Parker, *Parkes*, and *Parkman* identified the ancestor who was a game warden in the fenced or hedged small woods of a king's or nobleman's estate. Such a "park" included deer and other wild animals. See *Forrester*, *Ryder*. Root: O.E. *pearroc* (park).

Parkes see *Parker*.

Parkman see *Parker*.

118

Ryder identified the ancestor who was the warden on horseback for a large royal game forest. He had to be an excellent archer as well as woodsman. See *Forrester, Ward, Parker*. Root: O.E. *rydere*.

Steadman and *Stedman* identified the ancestor who was an expert with horses. Root: O.E. *stede* (steed or horse). See *Marshall*.

Stedman see *Steadman*.

Stoddard identified the ancestor who was in charge of horses used for breeding. Root: O.E. *stod* (breeding horse) and *weard* (guard or keeper).

Tiller and *Tillman* identified the ancestor who was a farmer. Root: O.E. *tilian* (to till, cultivate, or farm). See *Ackerman*.

Tillman see *Tiller*.

Ward(e) identified the ancestor who worked as a watchman or warden in a fortress or in a forest. *Warner, Warren,* and *Warriner* are variations. Root: O.E. *weard* (guard, protector, or watchman).

Warner see *Ward(e)*.

Warren see *Ward(e)*.

Warriner see *Ward(e)*.

Woodgate identified the woods gate-keeper.

Woodard and *Woodward* identified the ancestor who herded swine in a woods or forest. Root: O.E. *wudu* (wood) and *hierde* (herder).

Woodman and *Woods* identified the ancestor who chopped trees in a woods or forest of a king or nobleman. Root: O.E. *wudu* (wood).

Woodruff identified the ancestor who was a protector of wild game in the woods of a king or nobleman. Root: O.E. *wudu* (wood) and *rofa* (guardian or protector).

Woods see *Woodman*.

Woodward see *Woodard*.

- OCCUPATION NAMES from the SHEEP and WOOL INDUSTRY -

Every region in medieval Britain had sheep farms. The importance of such an industry gave us today's various "sheep" family names: *Lamb, Lambert, Lambden, Lamkin, Lambton, Ramsdale, Ramsden, Ramsey, Shapcot, Shapton, Shapey, Shapell, Shepherd, Shepley, Shipley, Shipman, Weatherall, Wetherell, Wetherby, Wetherspoon,* and *Withers*.

During the eleventh and twelfth centuries wool was not graded by the special breeds of sheep. It was judged excellent or poor according to the countryside it came from. The best quality of wool fiber in those years came from the districts of Shropshire, Herefordshire, and Cotswold. The special breeding of sheep for high quality was the concern of monks in monasteries during the thirteenth century throughout England.

Weavers of wool usually lived in villages near sheep herds, and they bought raw wool at sheep shearing time. They carried this raw wool to their village cottages where they spun and wove unfinished cloth from such sheep shearings. Buyers from towns nearby bought this raw cloth, transporting it back to town where dyers and finishers prepared such raw cloth for final sale.

From the fourteenth to the twentieth century Britain was the largest cloth manufacturer in the world. Two of its best known textiles are: Worsted and Jersey.

120

WORSTED identifies the town of Worstead, in Norfolk County most famous for its excellent woolen fabrics chiefly used in suits, coats and sweaters.

JERSEY is a close-knitted soft woolen cloth that made the Scottish island of Jersey famous for this wool textile. JERSEY long ago was a special type of woolen material used for seamen's sweaters and shirts. By 1900 A.D. this same jersey cloth was a feature for athlete's clothing.

Burrell identified the ancestor who was a weaver of burel, a wool cloth that was stiff and rough yet warm to the body. It was the cheapest woolen material in the Middle Ages, used by peasants and poor friars. Root: O. Fr. *burel.*

Callander identified the ancestor who operated a medieval calender (a roller for smoothing wool cloth). Root: O. Fr. *calandre* (calender).

Carde(r) identified the ancestor who carded wool, a process of separating the wool fibers to prepare the wool for spinning into cloth. Root: O. Fr. *carder* (to card).

Dexter is a name for a female dyer. See *Dyer, Baxter.*

Dresser and *Dressler* identified the ancestor who "dressed" woolen cloth by removing lumps and knots from unfinished woolen textiles, creating a smooth nap on this woolen material. Root: O. Fr. *dresser.*

Dressler see *Dresser.*

Dreyer identified the ancestor who dried cloth after it had been washed. Root: O.E. *drygean* (to dry).

Dyer identified the ancestor who dyed cloth. *Dyster* identified a female dyer. *Dexter* was a variation. Root: O.E. *doagere* (dyer).

Dyster see *Dyer*.

Flaxman identified the ancestor who made and sold flax cloth. Root: O.E. *fleax*.

Lander(s) see *Lavender*.

Lavender identified the ancestor who gave woolen cloth its final washing and bleaching. Root: O. Fr. *lavendier* (washer). *Lander(s)* and *Landry* are variations.

- - - - - - - - - -

Why do we say DENIM? A cotton material of strong twisted fibers was imported into England from the French town of *de Nimes* (pronounced day Neem). The English pronounced it as DENIM.

- - - - - - - - - -

Landry see *Lavender*.

Lister is from the Old English *litte* (dyer). See *Dyer*.

Lyster see *Lister* and *Baxter*.

Mercer identified the ancestor or who was a merchant of fancy, expensive cloth. Only the wealthy could afford to buy his silks, velvets, or imported woolens. *Mercer* always was one of the wealthy persons in his town. Root: from O. Fr. *mercier* (merchant).

Packard identified the ancestor who packed wool into large bundles for shipment. Root: O.E. *packe* (to pack for shipment).

Packer see *Packard*.

Plunkett identified an ancestor who made and sold "plunket" cloth, a textile that was gray, coarse, unbleached, and undyed. It was "poor peoples' cloth". Root: O. Fr. *plonkie* (plunket).

Scherer see *Shearer*.

Sharman see *Shearer*.

Shearer and *Shearman* identified the ancestor who was a skilled cutter of cloth. Root: O.E. *sceran* (to shear or cut).

Shears see *Shearer*.

Shearsmith. A scissors is two knife blades securely fastened to form a sharp-cutting tool that became an indispensable item once it was invented. Special modern machinery today produces excellent shears for home or industrial use. The handmade scissors made by medieval smiths must have been excellent also, for Britain's early textile industry depended on good shears. *Shearsmith* was the byname for the smith who specialized in making scissors of all sizes.

Sherman see *Shearer*.

Shepard, *Sheper*, *Shephard*, *Shepherd*, *Sheppardson*, *Shepperson*, and *Shipperson* identified the ancestor who was a "keeper" of sheep. His job was to keep wolves from attacking the sheep. Root: O.E. *sceap* (sheep) and *hirde* (herder).

Sheper see *Shepard*.

Shephard see *Shepard*.

Sheppardson see *Shepard*.

Shepperson see *Shepard*.

Shipperson see *Shepard*.

Shurman see *Shearer.*

Tessler identified the ancestor who was very skilled in the final stage of cloth production. The *Tessler* finished a wool textile by carefully raising a nap on its surface. Root: O.E. *taesel* (nap).

Tucker is from the Old English *tucian* (to thicken by stomping on cloth). See *Fuller, Walker.*

Walker identified the ancestor who worked as a fuller of cloth. Finished raw wool textile had to be cleaned and thickened (fulled) before it could be dyed. A cleansing agent called "fuller's earth" was put into a large trough of water in which raw wool cloth was soaking. A barefooted workman walked back and forth on this raw textile to remove dirt and to cause the cloth to thicken. In some districts a *Walker* was called a *Fuller* or a *Tucker.* It is estimated that over 500,000 *Walkers, Tuckers,* and *Fullers* live in the U.S.A. That gives us some idea of the many medieval ancestors who made their daily living "walking" on raw wool cloth. Root: O.E. *fullere* (to thicken).

Weathers and *Wethers* identified the ancestor who was a sheepherder for a flock of yearling rams (lambs that were castrated before they fully matured).

Weaver see *Webber.*

Webber identified the ancestor who worked as a weaver. Clothmaking during the Middle Ages was a cottage industry. Most weavers spun and wove textiles at home. Their cottages also served as a shop which sold cloth. Root: O.E. *webbe* (to weave).

Webster identified a female weaver. See *Webber, Baxter.*

Wethers see *Weathers.*

Withers see *Weathers*.

Woolfolk identified the ancestor who worked in a large shop where wool was woven. Root: O.E. *wull* (wool) and *folc* (peasant).

Woolman identified the ancestor who sold wool in a town shop. Root: O.E. *wull* (wool) and *mann* (man). Occasionally a *Woolman* also identified a servant for a wool-merchant.

CHAPTER 5

35% of our FAMILY NAMES
come from FIRST NAMES OF PARENTS

In 1066 A.D. William the Conqueror and his Norman-French army invaded and gained possession of the British Isles. This military conquest changed the naming customs of the British people. The French language quickly replaced Anglo-Saxon ways of speech and writing. A new style of personal or first names gradually was accepted by the conquered Anglo-Saxons. During the first fifty years of Norman-French government most of the original Anglo-Saxon names disappeared.

Below are a few Anglo-Saxon names that survived the Norman conquest of 1066 A.D. These American family names listed below remind us of the many spelling and pronunciation changes during nine hundred years of history (from 1066 A.D. until today):

U.S.A FAMILY NAMES	ANGLO-SAXON FIRST NAMES
Aldrich	Aleuric
Havelock	Aseloc
Black	Blaec
Brodie	Brodo
Browning	Bruning
Knight	Cniht
Crooke	Cruk
Couts	Couta
Fellows	Folaga

127

Goodman	Godmund
Goodrich	Godric
Green	Grene
Grant	Grente
Leaman	Leofman
Leveson	Leofsun
Merritt	Maergeat
Norman	Northman
Osborne	Osbeorn
Osgood	Osgot
Raynor	Ragnar
Seaward	Siewaerd
Sewell	Sigeweald
Thurston	Thurstan
White	Hwita
Willard	Ulivard
Wyburn	Wigbeorn
Wolsey	Wulfsige
Woolford	Wulfweard

By 1150 A.D. the French language of the Normans had established new customs for British people. The earlier English (Anglo-Saxons) now used the Norman-French naming system when they baptized their babies. Below is a list of popular Norman-French names for babies which the Anglo-Saxons (English) imitated by 1150 A.D.:

William	Alice
Robert	Maud
Richard	Adela
Geoffrey	Margery
Henry	Rosamund
Hugh	Muriel
Ralph	Olive
Gilbert	Emma
Thomas	Yvonne
Walter	Matilda

Name lists of British churches and government records show the popularity of the following first names for English male babies by 1200 A.D.

```
     William (15%)        Richard (11%)
     Robert (12%)         Henry (10%)
```

Such percentages show the need in the Middle Ages for a second name of identification. So:

Robert's son William became William son of Robert or William *Robertson*.

Peter's son Richard became Richard son of Peter or Richard *Peterson*.

Not all "son" names are rooted in a father's first name. Below are examples of some American family names that are rooted in the mother's first name:

```
 *Addison - son of Addie (Adela)
  Amison - son of Amicia (Amy)
  Annison - son of Agnes
  Anson - son of Anne
 *Babson - son of Babs (Barbara)
  Belson - son of Belle
  Bettison - son of Bettie
  Betson - son of Beatrice
  Casson - son of Cassandra
  Catherson - son of Catherine
  Catterson - son of Catherine
  Cristison - son of Christine
 *Denison - son of Denise
 *Edison - son of Edith
  Edson - son of Edwina
  Ellenson - son of Ellen
  Ellison - son of Ella
  Eveson - son of Eve
  Evison - son of Eve
  Gillson - son of Jill (Gillian)
  Gilson - on of Gill (Gillian)
  Ibbotson - son of Ibbo (Isobel)
  Janison - son of Jane
  Jennison - son of Jennie
  Kateson - son of Katherine
  Kitson - son of Kit (Kitty)
```

```
      Mabson - son of Mabb (Mabel)
      Magson - son of Marge
      Malleson - son of Malley (Molly)
      Margeson - son of Margaret
     *Matson - son of Matilda
      Mawson - son of Matilda
      Mollison - son of Molly (Mary)
      Moxon - son of Mogg (Marge)
     *Nelson - son of Nell
      Nellison - son of Nellie
      Sibson - son of Sybil
      Tillotson - son of Tibb (Isobel)
```

*Also a root for male family names.

- WHO KNOWS?
SOMEDAY IT JUST MIGHT HAPPEN -

One of our radio or TV stations might announce
the following news item:

"A British TV station in London today reported that
salvage divers have located the remains of a fourteenth century sailing ship that sank in the English
Channel more than five hundred years ago during a
severe storm. It was named the *Pride of London*.

"The British Registry of Shipping stated that this
wrecked ship departed for Lisbon, Portugal, on
March 12, 1386, with a cargo of woolen textiles and
metal products.

"The *Pride of London* apparently was returning to
London when an intense storm sank the ship in the
English Channel near the mouth of the Thames
River. Its cargo contained Portuguese wine and
many silver bars from Spanish mines. These silver
bars could be worth millions of British pounds.

"Captain Edward Adams of Liverpool owned the
Pride of London. Possible *Adams* heirs to this
ship's cargo of silver, etc. are advised to contact
her majesty's admiralty port office in London."

Following are twenty-six family names that have roots in the ancestral name of *Adams*. These persons might easily prove how their family names became changed or varied through nine hundred years of family histories:

Adcock	Adhams	Atkin
Adcox	Adie	Atkins
Adamson	Adkins	Atkinson
Addams	Adkinson	Hadcock
Addamson	Aitkin	Macadams
Ade	Aitkins	Mac Adams
Addeson	Aitkinson	Mac Adies
Addison	Akens	
Addyman	Akins	

These variations represent more than 500,000 *Adams* descendants who are listed in our phone books. Therefore it's a good guess that at least 600,000 American and British persons with *Adams* name roots possibly could claim to be "heirs" to the cargo treasure of the *Pride of London*!

- FAMILY-NAME FOSSILS from
FIRST NAMES of FATHERS or MOTHERS -

Alexander

Root: *Alexander* was a Greek name meaning "helper of people". This had always been a very popular name in Europe for royalty and noblemen; its Russian nickname was Sasha. Sander and Saunder were a fast Scottish pronunciation for Alexander. Pioneer Scottish settlers made the name popular in America (as Alec or Alex) until about 1850. Sandra is a female variation from Alexandra.

This name came to England with William the Conqueror. The French pronounced it "Al-i-saundre", but the English and Scottish people said "Alister, Alistar, Alick, Ellic, Alec, and Saunder". The Scots invented the famous nickname of "Sandy" for a lovable Scot.

Phonebook Name Fossils

Alexander – one of the
  most common versions
Callister
Collister
Macalaster
Saunder
Saunders – one of the
  most common versions
Saunderson

MacAllister
Sander
Sanderlin
Sanders
Sanderson

Alexander in other places:

Alexandros and Alexandropoulos (Greece)
Allesandro and Allesio (Ital.)
Alejandro and Alejo (Span.)
Alexandre and Aleiko (Port.)
Alexandre and Alexis (Fr.)
Alesander (Ger., Scan.)
Alexi, Alescha, and Sascha (Russ.)

Anson

Root: *Anson* identified the ancestors Agnes and Ann. Agnes is from a Greek work meaning "the outstanding one". During the Middle Ages it usually was one of three top popular female names. Agnes was pronounced Annis in medieval times.

Ann(e) is from the Hebrew Hannah, meaning "born with God's blessing". As a Bible name Hannah (Anna) is over three thousand years old. Nancy was a Middle Ages nickname for Ann.

Phonebook Name Fossils

Annas   Annis
Anness   Annison

Anne in other places:

Annette and Nanett (Fr.)   Nani (Hung.)
Hanne (Ger.)   Anna and Ninetta (Ital.)
Antje and Naatje (Da.)   Anna and Annika (Dan.)
Anninka (Russ.)   Aneta (Yugo.)

St. Agnes was the patron saint of romantic-minded young ladies of the Middle Ages. They idolized St. Agnes as a youthful and innocent martyr. Many legends were told about this saint's purity of thought and behavior. On the holiday of St. Agnes' Eve unmarried English ladies often celebrated with a private festival that included a secret ceremony that was supposed to give each maiden a clue or even a vision of a future husband.

Agnes in other places:

Agni (Greek)   Agnes (Hun.)
Agnessa (Bulg.)   Agnesea (It.)
Agnieszka (Pol.)   Ines (Port., Span.)
Anuska (Czech.)   Ynez (Port., Span.)

Bartholomew

Root: *Bartholomew* was a Hebrew name meaning "the farmer's son". One hundred and sixty-five English churches and one religious holiday have been named for this popular medieval saint. It was sometimes spelled "Bartelmy" in medieval days. "Partholomaeus" was its Latin form.

Phonebook Name Fossils

Bartell   Bartley
Barth   Bateman
Bartholomay   Bates – a
Bartman   common version
Bartle   Bateson
Bartlett – a   Battison
  common version

133

Bartholomew in other places:

Bartek (Pol.)	Bartholome (Fr.)
Bartos (Czech.)	Bartolomeu (Port.)
Bartok (Hung.)	Bartolome (Span.)
Bartel (Dan.)	Bartolomeo (Ital.)
Bartholoaus and	Bartholomaios (Greek)
Barthel (Ger.)	

Bridget

Saint Bridget was "Patroness of Ireland", making Bridget a best beloved name. Mythologically, Irish "Bridhid" was goddess of fertility, fire, wisdom, and the arts. Saint Bergetta of Sweden was a cognate for Irish Bridget ("the noble and enlightened one"). By the fifteenth century Bridget was almost as popular in Ireland as Mary was. Nineteenth century English dramatists stereotyped Bridget as a simpering kitchen helper or chamber maid, thereby demeaning the Middle Ages "nobleness" of her Irish origin and esteem.

Bridget in other places:

Brigida (Ital., Span.)	Berek (Greek)
Brigitte (Fr.)	Brygitka (Pol.)
Brigita (Czech., Russ.)	Birgitta (Swed.)

Catterson

Root: *Catterson* identified the "son of Catherine". It was spelled with a "K" in medieval days, slowly changing to Catherine by 1600 A.D. Saint Katherne was a Grecian maiden who was executed in 307 A.D. because she had converted to Christianity.

The early Crusaders brought the name Katherine to medieval England. This name came from the Greek word Katharos meaning "the person without sin".

Catherine in other places:

Katerina (Bulg.)

Katka (Czech.)

Catherine, Caron (Fr.)

Catalina (Span., Port.)

Katrina (Ger.)

Kati (Hun.)

Caterina (Ital.)

Katarzyna (Pol.)

Katinka (Russ.)

Colson

Root: *Cole*, *Collins*, and *Clason* are shortened names from the longer Greek name of *Nicholas*, meaning "champion of the common people".

Throughout Europe during the Middle Ages, St. Nicholas was the lovable patron saint of children and sailors. (See *Nicholson*.)

Phonebook Name Fossils

Cole (Eng.)

Coleman (Eng.) - a common version

Coles (Eng.) - one of the most common versions

Coleson (Eng.)

Collett (Eng.)

Collette (Eng.)

Colley (Welsh, Eng.)

Collin (Eng.)

Collings (Eng.)

Collinson (Eng.)

Collison (Eng.)

Colman (Irish)

Clason (Scot.)

Clayson (Scot.)

Clowles (Eng.)

Davidson

Root: *David* is from the Hebrew language; it was an ancient lullaby word meaning "dear little one". The patron saint of ancient Wales was David, an archbishop in Wales in the sixth century (St. Dawfydd). The early Irish form was "Dathi".

Taffy was a medieval nickname for David. Since 1950 A.D. David, as a first name in America, has usually ranked among the top five popular first names.

Phonebook Name Fossils

Davis (Welsh, Scot.)
Davies (Welsh)
Davis (Eng., Welsh) - the
  most common version
Davison (Eng.)
Dewey (Welsh, Scot.)

Dawes (Welsh)
Dawkins (Welsh)
Dawson (Eng.)
Deak (Welsh)
Deakin (Welsh)
MacTavish (Scot.)

David in other places:

David (Fr., Ger.,
  Greece, Heb.)
Daveed (Russ.)
Dake (Yugo.)
Davidah (Isr.)

Tadlis (Rom.)
Tavis (Welsh)
Davde (Ital.)
Dawid (Pol., Port.,
  Span., Swed.)

Ellison

Root: *Ellison* identified "the son of Ellis or Elijah". Elijah, meaning "Jehova is my God", was a popular Bible name in the Middle Ages. Elias was the Grecian version for Elijah.

Although popular as a first name in New England in the 1880s, Elijah has now almost disappeared in America.

Phonebook Name Fossils

Elias (Eng.)
Elkins (Eng.)
Ellert (Eng.)
Eliot (Eng.)
Elliot (Eng.)
Elliott (Eng.) - a common
  version

Elkinson (Eng.)
Ellis (Eng.) - a
  common version
Ellison (Eng.)

Ellison in other places:

Elia (Ital.)
Elias (Port., Span.,
  Nor., Ger., Den.)

Eliasz (Pol.)
Elie (Fr.)
Elihu (Swed.)

```
    Ilias (Greek)           Iliia (Bulg.)
            Iluah (Yugo.)
```

FitzAlan . . . FitzHenry . . . FitzHugh

Norman-French lords and ladies identified their sons
as "fils de Alan", "fils de Hugh", etc. It was a
French aristocratic identification meaning "son of
----".   Twelfth century English lords and ladies
quickly imitated this French-naming custom.   The
French pronunciation for fils (son) was feese.   The
English nobles spelled and pronounced "fils" as
"fitz".

Near the end of the thirteenth century several
Norman-French noblemen settled in Ireland.   Many
Irish nobles also copied the "fitz" naming for their
sons.

FRENCH	ENGLISH, IRISH
FitzAlan – fils de Alan =	son of Alan
FitzHenry – fils de Henry =	son of Henry
FitzHugh – fils de HUGH =	son of Hugh

Gilbertson

Root: *Gilbertson,* meaning "child of great hope",
identified "the son of Gilbert".   It was a Norman-
French name that must have been very popular in
medieval days as is indicated by its thirteen family-
name variations.

Gilbert has been a somewhat common first name in
America.

Phonebook Name Fossils

Gibbons (Eng.)	Gilman (Eng.)
Gibbs (Eng.)	Gilson (Eng.)
Gibson (Eng.)	Gipps (Eng.)
Gilbert (Eng.) – the most	Gipson (Eng.)
common version	FitzGilbert (Ir.)

Gilbert in other places:

Gilpin (Du.)   Guilbert (Fr.)
Gilberto (Span., Ital.,   Gilbertus (Latin)
  Port., Ger.)   Gwalberto (Pol.)
Gilbert (Swed., Nor., Dan.)

Gregson

Root: The Greek word *gregorious* (Gregory) meant "the watchful and alert one". The name of Gregory is memorialized by sixteen popes, some Gregorian religious music, and by today's Gregorian calendar.

Gregory was never popular in America as a first name.

Phonebook Name Fossils

Gregg (Eng.)   Grierson (Scot.)
Greggs (Eng.)   Griggs (Eng.)
Gregory (Scot.)   Grigson (Eng.)
Greig (Scot.)   MacGregor (Scot.)
Grier (Scot.)

Gregory in other places:

Gregoire (Fr.)   Gregoor (Dan.)
Gregorio (Span.,   Gregor (Ger.)
  Ital., Port.)   Griseha (Russ.)
Grega (Czech.)   Grigori (Bulg.)
Gregorich (Yugo.)   Gregorious (Greece)
Grzegorski (Pol.)

Harrison

Root: *Harrison*, meaning "chieftain of a fortress or an enclosed estate", identified the "son of Harry or Henry".

The Norman-French brought the name of Henri to England, pronouncing it as "Awn-ree". The Anglo-

Saxons omitted the "n", pronouncing Henri as Harry. Old Welsh or Gaelic "ap Harry" (son of Harry) soon blended into Parry and Perry.

Phonebook Name Fossils

Harkins (Eng.)
Harriman (Eng.)
Harris (Eng.) - one of
  the most common versions
Harrison (Eng.)
Hawes (Eng.)
Hawkes (Eng.)
Hawkins (Eng.)
Hawkinson (Eng.)
Henderson (Scot.) - one of
  the most common versions

Hendries (Scot.)
Hendry (Scot.)
Henkins (Eng.)
Henries (Eng.)
Henry (Eng.)
McHenry (Irish)
Parry (Welsh)
Perry (Welsh)

Henry in other places:

Henrick and
  Heintz (Ger.)
Enzio and
  Enrico (Ital.)
Enrique (Port., Span.)
Herriot and Henri (Fr.)
Hendrik (Dan.,
  Nor. Swed.)

Heintje and
  Hendrik (Du.)
Heinricus and
  Enricas (Latin)
Jindrich (Czech.)
Henrim (Bulg.)

Hugh

Name-fossils can be explained as traces or remains of identifications of early ancestors. The Norman-French name of Hugh was misspelled and mispronounced by the English. Nine hundred years of English language have changed Hugh into:

Hewe	Howe	Hues	Hutchins
Hewes	Howes	Huey	Hutchinson
Hewson	Howie	Hughes	Hutchison
Hewitt	Howlett	Hutchens	
Hewlett	Howson	Hutcheson	

Jefferson

Root: *Jefferson* identified the "son of Jeffrey". The French brought it to England as Geoffroi in 1066 A.D. where it later became Godfrey.

By 1300 A.D. this name was spelled Jeffrey. Jeff and Jeffrey have become quite popular in America since World War II.

Phonebook Name Fossils

Jefferies (Eng.)	Jeffery (Eng.)
Jeffers (Eng.)	Jeffries (Eng.)
Jefferson – the most	Jeffrey (Eng.)
common version	Jephson (Eng.)

Jeffrey in other places:

Jeffrol and Jofre (Fr.)	Govert (Du.)
Gottfried (Ger.)	Gotfryd (Pol.)
Goffredo and	Gotfrid (Russ.)
Giotto (Ital.)	Bogomir (Yugo.)
Gofredo and	
Gofreto (Span.)	

Lawrence

Root: *Lawrence* is from the Latin *laurentius* (the champion or the victorious one). St. Laurence's name has been honored by two hundred and thirty-seven churches in England, indicating his popularity during the Middle Ages. Since Laurence was a non-bibical saint, the Puritans shunned his name.

In ancient Greece the sacred laurel tree was regarded as a symbol of Apollo. Winners of poetry or athletic contests were "championed" (laurel-leafed) with a wreath of leaves from a laurel tree.

Martyred St. Laurencius (258 A.D.) was extremely popular in Ireland where he was regarded as a unique religious champion of blind and deformed persons. British monks sometimes renamed themselves "Laurence" soon after taking up residence in a monastery.

Phonebook Name Fossils

```
Larkin (Eng.)
Laurence (Welsh) - the preferred spelling in Great
     Britain
Laurie (Scot.)
Lawrence (Eng.) - one of the most common versions
Lawrie (Scot.)
Lawson (Eng.) - one of the most common versions
Lowry (Scot.)
```

Researcher Elsdon Smith has reported there are over 100,000 *Lawrences* in America.

Lawrence in other places:

```
Laurentius (Latin)          Orencz (Hung.)
Lorenzo (Ital., Span.)      Lavrentij (Russ.)
Lorencho (Port.)            Lovre (Yugo.)
Laurent (Fr.)               Wawrznlak (Pol.)
Lauritz (Dan.)
Larse and Lars (Nor.,
  Swed.)
```

Mc . . . Mac

Many Americans believe that Mc identifies an Irishman, and that Mac identifies a Scotsman. This is not true. Mc is simply an abbreviation of Mac, and Mc may identify an Irishman or a Scotsman - and the same is true of Mac.

The McGregor clan were considered to be an outlaw group in fifteenth century Scotland. In 1603 A.D. the Scottish Privy Council passed a law that abolished the name of McGregor. A McGregor was required to change his name or be executed. However, in 1661 A.D. King Charles II cancelled this anti-McGregor ruling, restoring the clan and its name to full citizenship status.

Scotland is famous for its long history of clans. Such a clan was a group of families or households that had a strong loyalty to the clan chieftain. When a Scotsman joined a clan, he took the clan's name as his family name.

The clan was a way of expanding a large tribe in order to protect themselves from their neighbors who might be - or might become - their enemies. Each member of a clan had a first name to identify himself from the other clan members.

The ancient Scottish or Gaelic Clann identified the ancestor member who was considered to be "a child of the brotherhood".

Mollison

Root: *Mollison* identified the son of Molly, a nickname for Mary, and Mary is from the Hebrew *Miriam* meaning "the bitter or sorrowful one". Maryom was the Arabic name form.

During the Middle Ages the name of Mary affectionately was used as Maryon or Marion (for example, Maid Marion of Robin Hood tales). In the sixteenth century Mary lost favor as a name because of the unpopularity of Queen "Bloody Mary" of Scotland. By the nineteenth century Mary once more became a common name for a girl. The nickname Polly (from Molly) possibly is an age-old trace of baby-talk pattern. Mally was a mispronunciation for Molly.

142

In the early Middle Ages in Spain, girls rarely were named Mary. Rather they were named for her life events or attributes such as: Dolores, Mercedes, Asuncion, and Concepcion.

Phonebook Name Fossils

Malkin	Marion
Mallen	Maris
Mallenson	Marison
Mallinson	Marriott

Mary in other places:

Marie and Manon (Fr.)	Morla and Maureen (Ir.)
Marya (Pol.)	Mair (Welsh)
Miriam (Heb.)	Mariska (Yugo.)
Mari and Marla (Ital., Span.)	Marla (Ger., Aus.)
	Marya and Masha (Russ.)

Nicholson

Root: *Nicholson* identified the son of Nicholas which is from the Latin Nicolaus meaning "the champion of the common people".

St. Nicholas was the patron saint of children, sailors, and pawnbrokers in Britain. The Puritans never used his name for their children because the Puritans disdained him as a non-biblical saint. The Dutch brought the Santa Claus tradition to America. However, Nicholas was never a popular given name in American colonial times. (See *Colson*.)

Phonebook Name Fossils

Nichol (Eng.)	Nickerson (Eng.)
Nicholas (Eng.) - one of the most common versions	Nicklas (Eng.)
	Nickles (Eng.)
Nicholl (Eng.)	Nicklous (Eng.)
Nichols (Eng.)	Nicoll (Scot., Welsh)
Nicholson - one of the most common versions	Nixon (Eng.)

143

Nicholas in other places:

Nicolo (Ital.)
Nicholas (Span.)
Nicolao (Port.)
Nikolaus (Greek)
Klaus and Niklas (Ger.)

Niklaas and Klasse (Du.)
Nicolaus and Nils (Dan.)
Nikolai (Russ.)
Mikula (Yugo.)

O'Brian - O'Brien - O'Brion
O'Bryan - O'Bryant

Root: In the tenth century King Brian of Ireland ruled that children of his chieftains should take their father's or grandfather's names and pass these names to their children. Thus the Irish favorite name style of *O'* (of) was invented. O'Brian means "descendant or grandson of Brian".

In 1485 A.D. the English Parliament passed this law: "Irishmen dwelling in the counties of Dublin, Myeth, Wriall, and Kildare shall gae apparelled like Englishmen, and ware their heads after English maner, sweare alegiance...and shall take to him an English surname of one town as Sutton, Chester, Trym, Spryne, Corke, or colour as Black, White or Browne and that he and his issue shall use this name under payne of forfeiting goods and land."

About 1750 A.D. Ireland came under strong control by English kings and noblemen. The Irish were pressured to drop this *O'* style of naming and often were required to take English types of names as identification.

144

However, by 1900 A.D., to show pride in their Irish heritage, some Irishmen used the old style *O'* for their names. By 1920 A.D. at least twenty per cent of Irish names used this *O'* name style which proudly said, "It's great to be the grandson of an Irishman."

Peterson

Root: Peter is from the Greek word *petros* meaning "one who is solid as a rock". Peter came to England from Western France as Pierre. By 1100 A.D. the Anglo-Saxons could only spell and say Pier (peer). By 1200 A.D. Peer and Piers were spelled and pronounced Peter and Peters. The Anglo-Saxons also had difficulty pronouncing St. Pierre (Peter) in French; they said it as Semper (St. Pierre). By 1260 A.D. the French name of "son of Pierre" became pronounced Piers, Pierce, and Pierson.

Churches used the Latin spelling Petrus (Peter) as a baptizing name. By 1250 A.D. Welsh pronunciation changed Petrus to Peters. St. Peter must have been a very popular Middle Ages apostle: 1,140 English churches were named for this favorite saint.

Phonebook Name Fossils

Parkins (Eng.)	Peary (Eng.)
Parkinson (Eng.)	Perk (Welsh)
Parkison (Eng.)	Perkins (Welsh)
Parlin (Eng.)	Perkinson (Welsh)
Parnell (Eng.)	Pernell (Eng.)
Pearce (Eng.)	Perrie (Scot.)
Pearson (Eng.)	Perry (Welsh, Eng.)
Peterkin (Eng.)	Petrie (scot.)
Peters (Welsh) – one of	Piers (Eng.)
the most common versions	Pierson (Eng.)
Peterson – one of the	
most common versions	

Peterson in other places:

Peterson – U.S.A.   di Pietro – Italy (de)
Peters – Wales   Petrescu – Romania
Pederssen – Scandinavia   Petrovich – Russia
Peturssen – Iceland   Petrowski – Poland
Poetersohn – Germany   Petrov – Bulgaria
Perez – Spain   Petropoulos – Greece

Richardson

Root: *Richardson* identified the son of Richard.   It
was   a   Norman-French   name   which   they   pronounced
Reeshard.   Some   name-historians   believe   it   means
"powerful ruler".   Others declare such a meaning to
be from uncertain facts.

King   Richard   the   Lion-Hearted   was   an   extremely
popular   ruler.   He   was   greatly   admired   for   his
battle   leadership   during   the   Third   Crusade   to   the
Holy   Land.   Richard   became   a   very   favorite   name
with   the   common   people.   The   limited   number   of
medieval,   male   first   names   caused   the   invention   of
rhyming   nicknames: Richard   was   abbreviated   into
Dick, Digg(s), Hick(s), or Rick.

Phonebook Name Fossils

Dickens (Eng.)   Hickox (Eng.)
Dickenson (Eng.)   Hicks (Eng.)
Dickerson (Eng.)   Hickson (Eng.)
Dickinson (Eng.)   Hitchcock (Eng.)
Dickson (Eng.)   Hitcheson (Eng.)
Diggens (Eng.)   Hixon (Eng.)
Dixon (Eng.)   Hudson (Eng.)
Dixson (Eng.)   Ickes (Eng.)
Hickey (Eng.)   Prichard (Welsh)
Pritchard (Welsh)   Rickardson (Eng.)
Richard (Eng.)   Rickerd (Eng.)
Richards (Eng., Welsh) –   Rickerts (Eng.)
  one of the most   Rickertson (Eng.)
  common versions   Ricketts (Eng.)
Richardson (Eng.) – one   Ritchard (Eng.)
  of the most   Ritchie (Scot.)
  common versions

146

Richard in other places:

Pritchard (Welsh)
Riikard (Du.)
Reichart (Ger.)
Ricardo (Port., Span.)
Richard (Fr.)
Riccardo (Ital.)

Rihard (Greek)
Rikard (Hung.)
Ryszard (Pol.)
Rostistlav (Russ.)
Rickard (Scan.)

Simonson

Root: *Simonson* identified the son of Simon, once a common Middle Ages first name, but it lost popularity after 1500 A.D. Perhaps the nursery rhyme "Simple Simon" made it unpopular. In the Greek language Simon meant the "snub-nosed one". From the Hebrew language it meant "the good listener".

Phonebook Name Fossils

FitzSimmons (Irish)
Simcock (Eng.)
Simcox (Eng.)
Simkins (Eng.)
Simmens (Eng.)
Simmond (Eng.)
Simmonds (Eng.)
Simmons (Eng.) - one of
 the most common versions
Simmunds (Eng.)
Simms (Eng.)
Simon (Eng.)
Simons (Eng.) - one of
 the most common versions

Simonson (Eng.)
Simpkins (Eng.)
Simpkinson (Eng.)
Simpson (Eng.)
Sims (Eng.)
Simson (Eng.)
Syme (Eng.)
Symes (Eng.)
Symington (Scot.)
Symmes (Eng.)
Symmons (Eng.)
Symonds (Eng.)

Simon in other places:

Jiminez (Span.)
Szymanski (Pol.)
Sienkiewicz (Pol.)
Shimon and Shimkus (Isr.)

Simeon (Fr., Ger., Heb.)
Simeone (Ital.)
Semon (Greek)
Senyushka (Russ.)

Thomas

Root: *Thomas* was a Hebrew word meaning "the twin". The ancient Greeks used this name as "Didymus" (the twin). Tom is usually preferred over Thomas as a first name in America.

Tommy, as a girl's first name (Tommy Jo, Tommy Ann, etc.) has been used chiefly in the southern states in America.

Phonebook Name Fossils

FitzThomas (Irish)
Tamblin (Scot.)
Tamblyn (Scot.)
Tamkin (Scot.)
Tamlyn (Scot.)
Tammas (Scot.)
Tamp (Scot.)
Tamplin (Scot.)
Thomas (Welsh) – one of
 the most common versions
Thomasson (Eng.)
Thome (Eng.)
Thompkins (Eng.)
Thompkinson (Eng.)
Thompson (Eng.) – a
 common version
Tolson (Eng.)
Tomblin (Eng.)
Tomes (Eng.)
Tomlinson (Eng.)
Tompkins (Eng.)
Tompkinson (Eng.)
Tompson (Eng.)
Tomsett (Eng.)
Tomson (Eng.)

Thomas in other places:

Thomsen (Scan.)
Masson (Fr.)
Toman (Czech.)
Tomaso and
 Maso (Ital.)
Tomas and Mazo (Span., Port.)
Tomczak (Pol.)
Foma (Russ.)
Thoma and Mass (Ger.)
Kyriakos (Greek)

- - - - - - - - - -

"Every Tom, Dick, and Harry" is a common expression from the Middle Ages, meaning "a person who was very ordinary, not worthy to be men-

148

tioned or remembered". "Tom, Tom, the piper's son" and "Little Tommy Tucker" were favorite medieval nursery rhymes. "Tom fool" referred to a medieval mentally retarded person, and "tomfoolery" meant "doing a silly or stupid action".

- - - - - - - - - -

Ever been curious about the phrase "peeping Tom"? An Anglo-Saxon legend of the ninth century relates the tale of Leofric, nobleman of Coventry, who imposed exorbitant taxes on his tenants. His wife, Lady Godiva, protested his greediness. Leofric challenged his wife to ride naked through the village's streets in exchange for his rescinding the harsh tax demands. She agreed to accept his proposal on the condition that all the citizens closed their house shutters and remained indoors while she rode unclad through the town. Leofric agreed. During the Lady's ride all shutters were closed except for those of tailor Tom. The legend maintains that Tom was blinded for violating Lady Godiva's public privacy and that Leofric reduced his tenants' taxes.

- - - - - - - - - -

Williamson

Root: William was the favorite first name in England until about 1600 A.D., having been brought to England by the Norman-French in 1066 A.D. This name originally was German (Willahelm), and it meant "powerful leader". William has been a most popular Christian first name, influenced by early princes, saints, and kings of the same name. Wil-

149

liam throughout the centuries has been a name chiefly for "the common man".

The French spelling and pronunciation for William is Guilliame (Gwee-yawm); Guillotine (the inventor of the dreaded beheading machine) was a French variation for William. The Welsh sometimes used Pulliam for William.

Phonebook Name Fossils

FitzWilliams (Eng.)
Gillman (Eng.)
Wilcock (Eng.)
Wilcox (Eng.)
Wilkes (Eng.)
Wilkie (Scot.)
Wilkins (Eng.)
Wilkinson (Eng.)
Willcock (Eng.)
Willets (Eng.)

Willett (Eng.)
Williams - one of the
  most common versions
Willis (Eng.)
Willmett (Eng.)
Wills (Eng.)
Willson (Eng.)
Wilson (Eng.) - a
  common version

William in other places:

Wille (Scan.)
Guilherme (Port.)
Guillermo (Span.)
Guglielmo (Ital.)
Willem (Du.)
Wilhelm (Ger.)

Guillaume (Fr.)
Vilko (Czech.)
Vasily (Russ.)
Boleslaw (Pol.)
Vasilios (Greece)

- - - - - - - - - -

Father calls me William
Sister calls me Will;
Mother calls me Willie,
But the fellers call be Bill!
    . . Eugene Field
  "Jest 'Fore Christmas"

- - - - - - - - - -

150

CHAPTER 6

40% of our FAMILY NAMES came from ADDRESS NAMES

- HOUSES had no ADDRESS NUMBERS in the MIDDLE AGES -

Peasants of the Middle Ages were keen observers of the geography where they lived. Any outdoor feature was often a special kind of landmark. Neighbors were usually identified by a hill, rock, well, swamp, building, or even a ditch near the place where the neighbor lived.

Such an address reference also became a second name for the neighbor.

Nine hundred years later our telephone books with family names of *Hill*, *Dale*, *Wells*, *Roche*, *Grove*, *Brooks*, *Woods*, and the like offer us clues and hints of the medieval landscape where some early ancestors once lived.

```
ANCESTOR                 ADDRESS

Atfield          lived at a field or meadow
Atgate           lived at or near an estate gate
Athill           lived at a place on a hill
Atkirk           lived at or near a church
Atlee            lived at or in a meadow
Attree           lived at a solitary tree
Atwater          lived at a lake or river
```

151

```
Atwell          lived at or near a well or spring
Atwood          lived at a place in a woods
Attaway         lived at the side of a road
Attridge        lived at a place on a ridge
```

The medieval church was often an ancestor's "address" identification. Thus *Church*, *Churchard*, (yard), *Churcher*, *Churchgate*, *Churchill*, *Churchman*, *Churchwell* were family names of ancestors who lived near, worked at, or came from a church address place.

Kirk is rooted in the Old Norman *kirkia* (church). Its special name usage in Scotland identified an ancestor who once lived in or came from:

```
Kirk            place of a church
Kirkbridge      place of St. Bride church
Kirkby          village with a church
Kirkham         village with a church
Kirkland        church estate
Kirkpatrick     church of St. Patrick
Kirkwood        woods of the church
```

- EAST - WEST - SOUTH - NORTH
ADDRESS NAMES -

The four directions of the compass were common identifications in the Middle Ages, a very sensible way of describing a location. North, South, East, or West often identified a direction "far, far away." At other times these compass directions identified an exact location in a settlement or village:

Eastwood identified the person who lived in a nearby woods easterly.

Estridge identified the ancestor who lived on a ridge in the east part of the settlement.

Escott identified the ancestor who lived in a cottage in the eastern part of the village.

Eastman identified the newcomer who once lived in an eastern district (man from the East).

Eston identified the ancestor who came from the village of Eston (settlement to the East).

Easley identified the ancestor who lived and worked in an eastern field of the village.

Westbrook identified the ancestor who lived and worked near a western brook of the village.

Westbury identified the newcomer who came from a "bury or borough" (fortified place) in a western district.

Wescott identified the ancestor who lived in a cottage in the western part of the village.

Weston identified the newcomer who once lived in Weston village.

Westley identified the ancestor who lived and worked in a field in the western part of the settlement.

Sutherland identified the ancestor who came from a place in southern Scotland.

Sudberry identified the ancestor who once lived in a "bury or borough" (fortified place in southern England).

Sutton identified the newcomer who came from the village of Sutton (southerly settlement).

Sudlow identified the ancestor who lived on a mound in the southern part of the village.

Norcutt identified the ancestor who lived in a cottage in the northern part of the village.

Northrop identified the ancestor who lived and worked on a farm in the northern part of the village.

Norton identified the newcomer who came from the village of Norton (northerly settlement).

Norris identified the newcomer from a northern region.

Norland identified the newcomer who came from a place in northern Scotland (the northlander).

Norwood identified the person who lived in a nearby woods to the north.

- ADDRESS FAMILY NAMES
from VILLAGE SHOP SIGNS -

Ancestors who lived in a village sometimes were named and identified from the nearest shop with a signboard. Since most Middle Ages ancestors were unable to read, all shops displayed a large signboard with a drawing. Thus a village ancestor could be named as follows:

ANCESTOR	ADDRESS
John BELL	lived near the shop sign of a bell
Tom SWAN	lived near the shop sign of a swan
Mary CROSS	lived near the shop sign of a cross
Gib ROEBUCK	lived near the shop sign of a deer
Alan LYONS	lived near the shop sign of a lion
Dick HARTE	lived near the shop sign of a deer
Guy STAGG	lived near the shop sign of a deer
Jill CONEY	lived near the shop sign of a rabbit

By 1200 A.D. most English ancestors had not yet acquired a family name. Thus twin brothers who lived in separate parts of a large village might have been known as "Roger atte ye signe of the locks and keye" (locksmith's shop) and "Harry atte ye signe of the stagg" (leather shop).

154

Misspellings and mispronunciation of medieval address names for ancestors listed below show how confusing it is today to figure out exactly what some of these names should mean:

The following names originated from people who lived and worked at a wheatfield: *Whatley, Whiteley, Whaton, Whitcraft, Whitten.*

The following names originated from people who lived and worked at a meadow wetland or at a wheatfield: *Whitacre, Whataker.*

The following names originated from people who lived at a sheep-covered slope (sheepherder): *Whitall, Whitehill.*

The following names originated from people who lived at a wet location: *Whitby, Whitly.*

The following names originated from people who lived and worked in a wide valley: *Whitcomb.*

The following names originated from people who lived at a white-flowered field: *Whitefield, Whitfield, Whittier.*

The following name originated from people who lived at a bald-surfaced slope: *Whitlow.*

The following names originated from people who lived and worked at a chalk-colored wasteland. *Whitmere*, *Whitmore*, *Whitney*.

The following name originated from people who lived at a place of white cottages: *Whittington*.

- BURG, BERRY, BOROUGH or BURY -

This medieval name-root-ending identified an ancestor's residence within a fortified place. Root: (for all below) O.E. *burh* (fort).

Newburg was an ancestor's home within a newly-built fort.

Presberry was a priest's home in a fortified place.

Pilsbury was the home of Pil who lived inside a fort.

Woodbury was an ancestor who lived within a wooden fort.

Stanborough was an ancestor who lived inside a stone fort.

- BY -

This medieval name-root-ending generally meant place or location of a homestead.

Crosby was an ancestor's home by a village cross or cross roads. Root: O.E. *cros*.

Kirby was an ancestor's home by a church. Root: O. Scot. *kirke* (church).

Rigsby was an ancestor's home on a ridge. Root: O.E. *hrvcg* (ridge).

Wetherby was an ancestor's home near the male sheep pens. Root: O.E. *widar* (male sheep).

156

Appleby was an ancestor's home near an apple orchard. Root: O.E. *aeppel* (apple).

- COT or COTT -

This medieval name-root-ending identified an ancestor's residence in a cottage.

Endicott was the ancestor who lived in the end cottage. Root: O.E. *cott* (cottage).

Walcott was the Welsh ancestor's cottage. Root: O.E. *cott.*

Prescott was the priest ancestor's cottage. Root: O.E. *cott.*

Westcott was the ancestor's cottage west of the castle or hall. Root: O.E. *cott.*

Caldecott was the ancestor whose cottage faced the cold wind. Root: O.E. *ceald* (cold).

- FORD -

This medieval name-root-ending identified an ancestor's residence at a river-crossing place.

Bradford was an ancestor's home by a wide stream or river. Root: O.E. *brad* (broad).

Oxford was an ancestor's home at a river crossing for oxen. Root: O.E. *oxa* (ox).

Burford was an ancestor's home at a river below a fort. Root: *burh* (fort).

Sandford was an ancestor's home at a sandy fording place.

Hartford was an ancestor's home at a deer fording place. Root: O.E. *heorot* (hart).

- HAM -

This medieval name-root-ending identified an ancestor's residence or homestead in an open space.

Bentham was an ancestor's home among heavy bent grass. Root: O.E. *beonet* (bent).

Burnham was an ancestor's home alongside a stream. Root: O.E. *burna* (stream).

Dunham was an ancestor's home on a hill. Root: O.E. *dun* (hill).

Farnham was an ancestor's home among wild fern. Root: A.S. *fearn* (fern).

Wareham was an ancestor's home near a fish trap or weir. Root: A.S. *waer* (dam).

- LEE, LEIGH, LEY, or LY -

This medieval name-root-ending described an ancestor's residence in a clearing inside a woods.

Oakley was an ancestor's home in an oak-tree clearing or field. Root: O.E. *ac* (oak).

Wrigley was an ancestor's home in a clearing below a ridge. Root: O.E. *hrvcg* or ridge.

Bradlee was an ancestor's home in a wide clearing. Root: O.E. *brad* (broad).

Raleigh was an ancestor's home in a red deer meadow. Root: O.E. *ra* (red deer).

Blakely was an ancestor's home in the blackwoods clearing. Root: O.E. *blaec* (black).

- PRIEST -

A priest's family name in medieval days often described where he lived or identified property he owned:

Presberry was the priest's estate.
Presby was the priest's residence.
Prescott was the priest's cottage.
Presley was the priest's farmstead.
Prestbury was the priest's enclosed residence.
Preston was the priest's home in a village.
Prestwick was the priest's dairy farm.
Prestwood was the priest's home in a woods.

- SWIN -

This medieval name-prefix-root identified an ancestor's residence at a pig farm.

Swinburne was an ancestor's home at a pig farm by a stream. Root: O.E. *burna* or stream.

Swinton was an ancestor's home in a swineherder's place.

Swindell was an ancestor's home at a pig farm in a valley.

Swinnard was an ancestor's home within a swineyard.

Swinbrook was an ancestor's home at the pig farm by the brook.

- TON -

This medieval name-root-ending identified an ancestor's residence or location in an enclosed area.

Dalton was an ancestor's home in a dale or valley. Root: A.S. *dahl* (valley).

Preston was an ancestor's home near the priest's house. Root: A.S. *proest* (priest).

Milton was an ancestor's home near a grain mill. Root: M.E. *mille* (mill).

Gatton was an ancestor's home near the goat pen. Root: O.E. *gat* (goat).

Fenton was an ancestor's home near a fen or swamp. Root: A.S. *fenn* (fen).

- WICK -

This medieval name-root-ending identified an ancestor's residence at a farm.

Goswick was an ancestor's home at a goose farm. Root: O.E. *gos* (goose).

Bewick was an ancestor's home at a bee farm. Root: O.E. *beo* (bee).

160

Cheswick was an ancestor's home at a cheese farm. Root: O.E. *cvs* (cheese).

Chadwick was an ancestor's home at Ceadda's farm place.

Hardwick was an ancestor's home at a sheep farm. Root: O.E. *heordewfc* (shepherd).

- APPLE -

In a typical Middle Ages settlement the manor house and the church usually were surrounded by small, crudely thatched cottages or huts. *Applegarth* "second-named" the ancestor with an apple tree in his garth (yard). Other "byname" identities were *Appleby* (lived near apple trees); *Applegate* (lived near the apple orchard gate); *Appleton* (place of a large apple orchard); *Applethwaite* (apple orchard in a new clearing); *Appling* (came from Applington village). *Appleman* was the vernacular reference to any of the above apple persons. Root: A.S. *appel* and O.E. *aepple*.

- ASH -

The English silver-barked ash tree often served as an outdoor pagan altar of worship (300-500 A.D.). Anglo-Saxons (700-1000 A.D.) shaped its tough wood into shining spears for their foot warriors. Later medieval architects used ash tree timber for framing roofs of large buildings. Ash "second-namings" included *Ashby* (lived at the ash grove); *Ashton* (ash tree village); *Ashford* (lived and worked at the ash tree river bank); *Ashmore* (lake border of ash trees); *Ashwood* (ancestor's home in the woods). *Ashman* was the vernacular way of identifying an "ash" ancestor. Root: O.E. *aesc* (ash tree).

- BRIDGE -

Bridgen and *Briggins* identified the person who lived at the end of a bridge.

161

Brigham identified the person who lived and worked near a bridge.

Brigsley identified the person who lived in a meadow near a bridge.

- ELM -

The Norman-French in 1066 A.D. found England to be largely a forest country. A squirrel could travel a long distance before touching ground in those times. The leafy branches of the stately elm, trees which usually grew at the fringes of a forest, made useful cattle food when grazing was limited. Throughout the ages the majestic elm tree has been a frequent symbol for English and American poets. In the Middle Ages elm often was a landscape "second name" of identification for an ancestor who lived and worked near elm trees: *Elme(s)* (at the elms); *Embleton* (near the village elm grove); *Emsley* (in the elm meadow); and *Elmhurst* (came from Elmhurst settlement). Root: O.E. *elm*.

- WOOD -

Greenwood identified the person who lived in woods full of tall grass.

Littlewood identified the person who lived in the nearby small woods.

Longwood identified the person who lived in the nearby extensive forest.

Sherwood identified a woods owned by the shire or county.

Woodard identified the woods swineherder.

Woodbridge identified the person who lived at the wooden bridge.

Woodfall identified the person who lived at fallen trees.

Woodford identified the person who lived at the woods river crossing.

Woodhead identified the person who lived at the upper woods.

Woodridge identified the person who lived at a wooded ridge.

CHAPTER 7

IF YOUR NAME ISN'T IN THIS BOOK

A search for surname information is always an uncertain process. Many of our family names have had several spelling changes these past hundreds of years. Surnames often were misspelled by immigration clerks; and the immigrating ancestor didn't dare correct such an important government official. Some immigrating ancestors changed the spelling of their names in order to adapt quickly to the language of their new country.

However, if you have patience and are willing to write one or more letters, you may have luck in your search for the meaning of your family name. Such a letter should always state that you seek only the meaning of your surname. Mention other possible spellings of your family name. (Check your telephone book and city directory for possible different spellings.)

There are three sources available to you to help you learn the meaning of your family name:

1. Family name dictionaries and books containing name information about ancestors in the British Isles (England, Wales, Scotland, and Ireland).

2. The Genealogical Society of the Church of Jesus Christ of Latter-Day Saints in Salt Lake City, Utah.

3. Genealogical societies in European countries other than the British Isles.

- FAMILY NAME SOURCE #1 -

If your ancestry originated in the British Isles (England, Wales, Ireland, or Scotland), there's a good possibility of finding information about the meaning of your surname.

Family-name books and dictionaries listed below can be found in most public, college, and university libraries in America.

Dictionary of American Family Names, by Elsdon C. Smith.
The Story of Our Names, by Elsdon C. Smith.
Our Names, by Eloise Lambert and Mario Pei.
Penquin Dictionary of Surnames, by Basil Cottell.
These Names of Ours, by A.W. Dellquest.
English Surnames, by Constance Mary Matthews.
Dictionary of British Surnames, by Percy Hide Reaney.

- FAMILY NAME SOURCE #2 -

The genealogical library of the Church of Jesus Christ of Latter-Day Saints has the most complete files of surname information in the world.

This Mormon family names center is internationally famous, and its services are free of charge. Be sure to include a self-addressed, stamped envelope when you write to:

Genealogical Dept. Library
50 West North Street
Salt Lake City, Utah 84150

It would be unreasonable to expect the above surname research center to have information about every person's family names. Yet, take a chance and write to them!

166

If your ancestry originated in a European country other than the British Isles, your chances of discovering the meaning of your surname are somewhat reduced. But don't be discouraged! Elsdon Smith's <u>Dictionary of American Family Names</u> has a good sampling of European surnames. You may also write to the Washington, D.C. Embassy of the country from which your ancestor migrated. State in your letter that you seek only the meaning of your family name and that you need the name and address of the official genealogical society for that particular country. Your use of English language will be no difficulty. Enclose a self-addressed, stamped envelope to the Embassy you contact.

When you write to a genealogical society in a foreign country, state that you desire to learn the meaning of your family name and include the international reply coupons which are available at your local post office. Be sure to enclose a self-addressed envelope and the above international reply coupons which is used as an international stamp.

Your local library should have a directory of embassy names and addresses in Washington, D.C.

Good luck in your family name search!

BIBLIOGRAPHY

Addison, Sir William, Understanding English Surnames. B.T. Batsford, London 1978.

Bardsley, Charles Wareing, English Surnames, Their Sources and Significations. Chatto and Windus, London 1889.

Baring-Bould, Sabine, Family Names and Their Story. Seeley and Co., London 1910.

Bowman, William Dodgson, The Story of Surnames. Gale Research Co., Detroit 1968.

Dellquest, Augustus Wilfrid, These Names of Ours. Thomas Y. Crowell Co., New York 1938.

Dolan, J.R., English Ancestral Names. Clarkson N. Potter, New York 1972.

Ewen, Cecil L'Estrange, A Guide To The Origin of British Surnames. John Gifford, London 1938.

Foreign Versions, Variations, and Diminutives of English Names. Published by the U.S. Government Printing Office for the U.S. Immigration and Naturalization Office 1973.

Freeman, J.W., Discovering Names. Shire Publications, Aylesbury, Bucks 1968.

Hassall, W.O., History Through Surnames. Pergamon Press, Oxford Univ Press 1967.

Lambert, Eloise and Mario Pei, Our Names. Lothrop, Lee, and Shephard, Inc., New York 1960.

MacLysaght, Edward, The Surnames of Ireland. Irish Univ. Press, Ireland 1969.

Matthews, C.M., English Surnames. Charles Scribner's Sons, New York 1966.

Reaney, P.H., Dictionary of British Surnames, 2nd edition. Routledge and Kegan Paul, London 1976.

Reaney, P.H., The Origin of English Surnames. Routledge and Kegan Paul, London 1967.

Smith, Elsdon C., American Surnames. Chilton Book Co., Philadelphia 1969.

Smith, Elsdon C., The Book of Smith. Nellen Pub. Co., New York 1978.

Smith, Elsdon C., Dictionary of American Family Names. Harper and Row, New York 1956.

INDEX

ANNA, 133
ANNAS, 132
ANNE, 13 132 133
ANNESS, 132
ANNETTE, 133
ANNIKA, 133
ANNINKA, 133
ANNIS, 132
ANNISON, 14 129 132
ANSON, 129 132
ANTJE, 133
ANUSKA, 133
APPLEBY, 157 161
APPLEGARTH, 161
APPLEGATE, 161
APPLEMAN, 161
APPLETHWAITE, 161
APPLETON, 161
APPLING, 161
APRIL, 20
ARCHER, 61 62
ARLOTT, 40
ARMOUR, 61
ARMSMITH, 105
ARMSTEAD, 61 62
ARMSTRONG, 11 41 55
ARROWSMITH, 95 105
ASELOC, 127
ASHBY, 161
ASHFORD, 161
ASHMAN, 161
ASHMORE, 161
ASHTON, 161
ASHWOOD, 161
ASUNCION, 143
ATFIELD, 151
ATGATE, 151
ATHILL, 151
ATKIN, 40 131
ATKINS, 40 131
ATKINSON, 131
ATKIRK, 151
ATLEE, 151

ATTAWAY, 152
ATTREE, 151
ATTRIDGE, 152
ATWATER, 151
ATWELL, 152
ATWOOD, 14 152
AULD, 41
AVERILL, 20
AXSMITH, 105
AYERS, 21
BABCOCK, 22
BABCOX, 22
BABSON, 129
BACHELOR, 61
BACON, 84
BADGER, 84
BAILEY, 77
BAILIE, 76
BAINES, 1 19 41
BAKER, 13 59 83 84
BAKESTER, 59
BALLARD, 11 13 17 41
BALLASTER, 61
BALLISTER, 62
BANNISTER, 84 87 99
BANNON, 41 56
BARBER, 62 85
BARBOUR, 62
BARHAM, 118
BARKER, 85 107
BARON, 6
BARRETT, 95
BARTEK, 134
BARTEL, 134
BARTELL, 133
BARTH, 133
BARTHEL, 134
BARTHOLOAUS, 134
BARTHOLOMAIOS, 134
BARTHOLOMAY, 133
BARTHOLOME, 134
BARTHOLOMEW, 133 134
BARTLE, 133

172

BODE, 62
BOGOMIR, 140
BOLER, 85
BOLESLAW, 150
BOLEYN, 6
BOLGER, 85 96
BOND, 111 112
BONNER, 21
BOOKER, 96 104
BOOTH, 5
BOSWELL, 6
BOTHAM, vi
BOTTOM, v vi
BOULGER, 85
BOULOGNE, 6
BOURNE, 1
BOURNES, 1
BOWER, 62
BOWERMAN, 60
BOWERS, 62
BOWLES, 13 85
BOWMAN, 62
BOWSMITH, 105
BOWYER, 62
BOYD, 43 56
BOYER, 62
BRADFORD, 8 158
BRADLEE, 159
BRASHEAR, 96
BREME, 4
BRENNER, 62
BRETONS, 2
BREWER, 86
BREWSTER, 8 86
BRIDGE, 78
BRIDGEMAN, 78
BRIDGEN, 112 161
BRIDGER, 111 112
BRIDGES, 78 112
BRIDGET, 134
BRIDGMAN, 111 112
BRIDHID, 134
BRIGGINS, 112 161

BRIGGS, 112
BRIGHAM, 112 162
BRIGIDA, 134
BRIGITA, 134
BRIGITTE, 134
BRIGSLEY, 112 162
BRISBANE, 21 63
BRITTANNIA, 2
BRITTERIDGE, 8
BROAD, 41 43
BROADHEAD, 19 43
BROADUS, 43
BRODIE, 127
BRODO, 127
BRONSON, 43
BROOK, 1
BROOKS, 1 151
BROUN, 43
BROWN, 8 41 43 47 52 55
BROWNE, 43
BROWNELL, 43
BROWNING, 43 127
BROWNSON, 43
BRUNING, 127
BRUNSON, 43
BRYGITKA, 134
BRYON, 11
BUCK, 44
BUCKLESMITH, 105
BUCKMAN, 60
BUGGS, iv v
BULLARD, 112
BULLITT, 19 44
BUNCHE, 13 44
BUNDY, 112
BUNKER, 21
BUNYAN, 44
BURFORD, 158
BURNAND, 21
BURNETT, 43
BURNHAM, 158
BURRELL, 121

BUSHELL, 96 99
BUTLER, 63
BUTTERMOUTH, 20
BYRD, 1 41 44
CACHIER, 78
CADDICK, 44
CADDOCK, 44
CADE, 44
CADWALLADER, 39
CAIRD, 97
CALDECOTT, 158
CALEY, 44
CALLANDER, 121
CALLISTER, 132
CALLOW, 44 45
CALLOWAY, 45
CALVERT, 112
CALVIN, 11 45 46
CAMBER, 86 87
CAMERON, 45
CAMM, 45
CAMMEL, 45
CAMPBELL, 1 45
CANDELIER, 6
CANNON, 78
CAPLAIN, 6
CAPP, 86
CAPPER, 86
CAPTAIN-BEAT-THE-BUSH, 40
CARDE, 121
CARDER, 121
CAREY, 43 45
CARNALL, 63
CARNELL, 63
CARON, 135
CARPENTER, 97
CARTER, 8 16 63 83
CARTWRIGHT, 97
CARVER, 8 97
CASSON, 129
CASTLE, 64
CASTLEMAN, 64

CATALINA, 135
CATCHER, 78 81
CATCHING, 64 69
CATCHINGS, 64 69
CATCHPOLE, 78
CATERINA, 135
CATHERINE, 134 135
CATHERSON, 129
CATSKIN, 20
CATTERSON, 134
CAUDELL, 22
CAULDCOTT, vi
CAULDWELL, 14 16
CECIL, 45
CEDRIC, 39
CHADWICK, 161
CHAFFE, 45
CHAFFIN, 45
CHALMERS, 64
CHAMBERLAIN, 64
CHAMBERS, 64
CHANCELLOR, 78
CHANDLER, 6 86
CHAPLAIN, 6
CHAPLIN, 64
CHAPMAN, 60 79
CHASE, 64
CHATMAN, 79
CHEEKS, 45
CHEESEMAN, 87 88 94
CHELTON, 8
CHERNOFF, 42
CHEROV, 42
CHESEMAN, 87
CHESLER, 87
CHESMAN, 87
CHESSEMAN, 86
CHESSICK, 14
CHESSMAN, 16 60
CHESTER, 2
CHESWICK, 87 161
CHEVALIER, 64
CHILDE, 22

CRIMMINS, 46
CRIPPS, 46
CRISP, 46
CRISPIN, 46
CRISTISON, 129
CRITCHET, 46
CROCKER, 88
CROCKETT, 11 46
CROKER, 88
CRONE, 43 46
CRONEN, 46 47
CRONIN, 43
CROOKE, 127
CROOKSHANKS, 47
CROSBY, 14 156
CROSS, 154
CROTTY, 47
CROWE, 47
CROWELL, 47
CRUIKSHANKS, 1 47
CRUILSHANKS, 47
CRUK, 127
CRUMP, 47
CULPEPPER, 88
CULVER, 23
CUMMINGS, 46 47
CURLEY, 46 47
CURTIS, 23
CURTOYS, 23
CUSHMAN, 65
CUSTER, 100
CUTHBERT, 39
CUTLER, 100
CUTTER, 1
CUYLER, 88 99
CZARNECKI, 42
CZERNY, 42
D'AUBIGNY, 6
D'ISIGNY, 6
DABER, 101
DABERMAN, 101
DABNEY, 6
DAKE, 136

DALE, vi 1 151
DALTON, 160
DARKE, 42 47
DATHI, 135
DAUBER, 101
DAVDE, 136
DAVEED, 136
DAVID, 23 135 136
DAVIDAH, 136
DAVIDSON, 135
DAVIES, 136
DAVIS, 136
DAVISON, 136
DAWBER, 101
DAWES, 136
DAWFYDD, 135
DAWID, 136
DAWKIN, 40
DAWKINS, 40 136
DAWSON, 136
DAY, 80
DEACON, 80
DEAGAN, 43 47
DEAK, 136
DEAKIN, 136
DEAN, vi 80
DEANE, 80
DEEKER, 113 114
DEEKS, 113 114
DEETCHER, 113 114
DEGUILLAUME, 6
DELL, vi
DENISON, 129
DEWEY, 136
DEXTER, 59 121
DEYKES, 113 114
DI PIETRO, 146
DICCON CRUIKSHANKS, 40
DICK, 146
DICKENS, 146
DICKENSON, 146
DICKERMAN, 113 114
DICKERS, 113 114

DICKERSON, 146
DICKINSON, 146
DICKMAN, 60 113
DICKSON, 146
DIDYMUS, 148
DIGG, 146
DIGGENS, 146
DIGGS, 146
DILLARD, 23
DILLER, 88
DILLMAN, 88
DILWORTH, 118
DINEEN, 43 47
DISNEY, 6
DISSHERE, 94
DIXON, 146
DIXSON, 146
DOBER, 101
DOBERED, 101
DOBERMAN, 101
DOGETAIL, 20
DOLAN, 42 47
DOLLING, 23
DOLORES, 143
DOMESOFT, 20
DONEGAN, 43 47
DONNE, 42 47
DOOLITTLE, 13 23
DORAN, 23
DOTEY, 8
DOTY, 48
DOUD, 42 48
DOUGHTY, 48
DOVE, 48
DOW, 42 48
DOWDY, 42 48
DOWLING, 23
DRAKE, 48
DRAPER, 1 88
DRESSER, 121
DRESSLER, 121
DREYER, 121
DRINKWATER, 24

DRIVER, 114
DROVER, 65
DU BOIS, iv
DU L'EAU, 6
DUFFIN, 42 48
DUKES, 61
DUNHAM, 158
DUNNE, 42 48
DURWARD, 65
DYER, 1 59 121 122
DYKES, 114
DYSTER, 59 121 122
EAGLE, 24
EAMES, 24
EARLY, 24
EASLEY, 153
EASTMAN, 153
EASTWOOD, 152
EATON, 8
EDISON, 129
EDSON, 129
EGAN, 24
EGBERT, 39
ELDER, 41 48
ELIA, 136
ELIAS, 136
ELIASZ, 136
ELIE, 136
ELIHU, 136
ELIJAH, 136
ELIOT, 136
ELKINS, 136
ELKINSON, 136
ELLENSON, 129
ELLERT, 136
ELLIC, 131
ELLICK, 7
ELLIOT, 136
ELLIOTT, 136
ELLIS, 8 136
ELLISON, 129 136
ELME, 162
ELMES, 162

ELMHURST, 162
ELMORE, 1
EMBLETON, 162
EMMA, 128
EMSLEY, 162
ENDICOTT, vi 14 157
ENGLISH, 8 24
ENNION, 24
ENNIS, 24
ENRICAS, 139
ENRICO, 139
ENRIGHT, 24
ENRIQUE, 139
ENZIO, 139
EOFOR, 4
ERNEST, 6
ESCOTT, vi 152
ESTON, 153
ESTRIDGE, 152
EVAN GOFF, 107
EVAN GOWAN, 107
EVESON, 129
EVISON, 129
EWART, 87 88
EYNON, 24
FAGAN, 24
FAIRCHILD, 48
FAIRFAX, 48 56
FALCON, 48
FALCONER, 65
FALK, 65
FALKNER, 65
FARMER, 114
FARNHAM, 158
FARRAR, 101 105
FARRIS, 101
FAUCONNIER, 6
FAULKNER, 6 65
FAYER, 48 56
FELAGA, 127
FELLOWS, 127
FENNELL, 88
FENTON, 160

FERMAGER, 86 88
FERMANGER, 86 88
FERRER, 101
FERRIS, 101
FIELDS, 1
FIL DE SIMON, 6
FINCH, 48
FINCHER, 114
FIRMAGER, 86 88
FIRMANGER, 86 88
FISHER, 101 114
FISHMAN, 61
FISK, 101
FITCH, 24
FITZ MAURICE, 42
FITZ MORRIS, 42
FITZALAN, 137
FITZGILBERT, 137
FITZHENRY, 137
FITZHUGH, 137
FITZMAURICE, 48
FITZMORRIS, 48
FITZSIMMONS, 6 147
FITZTHOMAS, 148
FITZWILLIAMS, 150
FLAXMAN, 122
FLETCHER, 8
FLOYD, 49
FLUTTER, 94
FLYNN, 49 54
FOMA, 148
FOOTE, 49
FORD, 1
FORREST, 114
FORRESTER, 114 115 119
FORWARD, 115
FOSTER, 25 115
FOURDON, 6
FOWLER, 65
FOX, 25
FOXX, 25
FREEMAN, 115
FRIQUWULF, 1

179

FROST, 25 49 56
FRYER, 101
FULLER, 1 9 124
FURMAGER, 86 88
GABLER, 80
GAINER, 49 56
GAIOLERE, 6
GAITHER, 115
GAITHERS, 115
GALBRAITH, 25 43 49
GALER, 65 66
GALLIGAN, 49 56
GALLOWAY, 25
GALT, 25
GALVIN, 49 56
GAMMON, 49
GANDY, 65
GARDENER, 66
GARDINER, 9
GARNER, 66
GARSON, 66
GATES, 14 16 66
GATTON, 160
GAULT, 25
GAYLER, 66
GAYLOR, 6 65-67
GAYLORD, 25
GAYNOR, 49 56
GEOFFREY, 128
GEOFFROI, 140
GERDNER, 66
GERRISH, 25
GEUFFROI, 6
GIBBONS, 137
GIBBS, 137
GIBSON, 137
GILBERT, 128 137 138
GILBERTO, 138
GILBERTSON, 137
GILBERTUS, 138
GILES CROOKLEG, 40
GILL, 25
GILLETTE, 6

GILLIGAN, 66
GILLMAN, 150
GILLSON, 129
GILMAN, 137
GILPIN, 138
GILSON, 129 137
GIOTTO, 140
GIOVANNI FEFFARO, 106
GIPPS, 137
GIPSON, 137
GITTINGS, 49
GLASS, 102
GLASSMAN, 102
GLEN, vi
GLOVER, 102
GOALER, 66 67
GODFREY, 140
GODMUND, 128
GODRIC, 128
GOFF, 102 105
GOFFREDO, 140
GOFORTH, iv v
GOFREDO, 140
GOFRETO, 140
GOLDSMITH, 102 105
GOLIGHTLY, 88 90
GOOCH, 49 54
GOOD, 25
GOODALE, 89
GOODBODY, 26
GOODCHILD, 26
GOODE, 26
GOODENOUGH, 26
GOODFELLOW, 26
GOODFRIEND, 26
GOODHART, 26
GOODHUE, 26
GOODHUGH, 26
GOODJOHN, 26
GOODKIN, 26
GOODMAN, 9 16 26 128
GOODRICH, 26 128
GOODSON, 26

GOODSPEED, 26
GOODWIN, 26
GOODYEAR, 26
GORDON, 6
GOSFIELD, 116
GOSFORD, 115 116
GOSLAND, 115 116
GOSLIN, 115 116
GOSS, 115 118
GOSSARD, 61 67 116
GOSSE, 115 118
GOSSERTT, 116
GOSWICK, 160
GOTFRID, 140
GOTFRYD, 140
GOTHARD, 16 116
GOTTFRIED, 140
GOUGH, 49 54 102
GOVE, 102
GOVERT, 140
GOW, 102
GOZZETT, 116
GRAME GAPETOOTH, 40
GRANGER, 67
GRANT, 49 128
GRAVENER, 89
GRAY, 50 52
GREEN, 128
GREENSMITH, 105
GREENWOOD, 162
GREGA, 138
GREGG, 138
GREGGS, 138
GREGOIRE, 138
GREGOOR, 138
GREGOR, 138
GREGORICH, 138
GREGORIO, 138
GREGORIOUS, 138
GREGORY, 138
GREGSON, 138
GREIG, 138
GRENE, 128

GRENTE, 128
GREY, 50
GREYSTONE, 15
GRICE, 50
GRIER, 138
GRIERSON, 138
GRIGGS, 138
GRIGORI, 138
GRIGSON, 138
GRISEHA, 138
GRISS, 50
GRISSEN, 50
GRISSIN, 50
GRISSOM, 50
GROSSCUP, 50
GROSVENOR, 67 76 89
GROVE, 151
GROVES, 1
GRZEGORSKI, 138
GUEST, 26
GUGLIELMO, 150
GUILBERT, 138
GUILHERME, 150
GUILLAUME, 150
GUILLERMO, 150
GUILLIAME, 150
GUILLOT, 6
GUILLOTINE, 150
GULLIVER, 26
GUNSMITH, 105
GWALBERTO, 138
GWINN, 50 56
GWYNN, 50 56
GWYNNE, 50
GYNN, 50 56
HACKER, 116
HADCOCK, 131
HAGGARD, 26
HAIRE, 116 117
HALDANE, 26
HALILIDAY, 26 27
HALL, 83
HALLMAN, 67

HAMMERSMITH, 105
HANCOCK, 22
HANNAH, 132
HANNE, 133
HARDER, 80 81 116
HARDRICK, 80 81
HARDWICK, 80 81 161
HARDY, 27
HARE, 117
HAREPYN, 20
HARFIELD, 117
HARGRAVE, 117
HARGRAVES, 117
HARGREAVES, 117
HARGROVE, 117
HARKINS, 139
HARLEY, 117
HARPER, 67
HARRIMAN, 139
HARRIS, 6 139
HARRISON, 138 139
HARRY, 138 139
HARTE, 154
HARTFIELD, 1
HARTFORD, 158
HASTEAD, 14
HAVELOCK, 127
HAWES, 139
HAWK, 50
HAWKE, 50
HAWKER, 59
HAWKES, 139
HAWKIN, 40
HAWKINS, 40 139
HAWKINSON, 139
HAWKSTER, 59
HAYES, 117
HAYWARD, 68 117
HEAD, 50
HEATH, 1
HEDGES, 1
HEFFERAN, 117
HEINRICUS, 139

HEINTJE, 139
HEINTZ, 139
HENDERSON, 139
HENDRIES, 139
HENDRIK, 139
HENDRY, 139
HENGEST, 4
HENKINS, 139
HENMAN, 89
HENRI, 138 139
HENRICK, 139
HENRIES, 139
HENRIM, 139
HENRY, 128 138 139
HERDER, 80
HERNAIS, 6
HERON, 50
HERRING, 89
HERRIOT, 6 139
HEWE, 139
HEWES, 139
HEWITT, 139
HEWLETT, 139
HEWSON, 139
HICK, 146
HICKEY, 146
HICKOX, 146
HICKS, 146
HICKSON, 146
HIDE, 118
HIGGENBOTTOM, vi
HILL, 1 151
HILLARY, 27
HILLMAN, 1
HINES, 68
HIRDMAN, 68 81
HITCHCOCK, 146
HITCHESON, 146
HIXON, 146
HOAO FERREIRO, 106
HOARE, 50
HOB O'THE HILL, 40
HOGG, 27

HOGGARD, 68
HOGGARTH, 68
HOGGE, iv v
HOLEBECK, 9
HOLLIDAY, 26 27
HOLLINS, 14
HOMER, 11
HOOD, 89
HOOPER, 102
HOPKIN, 40
HOPKINS, 9 40
HORNBLOWER, 68
HORNER, 86 87 89
HOWARD, 68 117
HOWE, 139
HOWES, 139
HOWIE, 139
HOWLAND, 9
HOWLETT, 139
HOWSON, 139
HUDSON, 146
HUES, 139
HUEY, 139
HUGH, 128
HUGHES, 139
HUNTER, 68
HUTCHENS, 139
HUTCHESON, 139
HUTCHINS, 139
HUTCHINSON, 139
HUTCHISON, 139
HWITA, 128
HYDE, 118
HYNES, 68
IABAJA TEMIRZI, 107
IAN GOW, 106
IBBOTSON, 129
ICKES, 146
ILIAS, 137
ILIIA, 137
ILUAH, 137
INES, 133
INGLIS, 27 28

INGLISH, 27 28
INGLISS, 28
INMAN, 61 90 92
INNES, 28
INNIS, 28
IOANNES SKMITON, 106
IOREMIERE, 103
IRELAND, 28
IRISH, 28
ISOBEL, 13
IVAN KOVAC, 106
IVAN KUZNETZOV, 106
JACKSON, 11
JAN KOVAR, 106
JAN KOWAL, 106
JAN SMID, 106
JANISON, 129
JANOS KOVACS, 106
JARMAIN, 28
JARMAN, 28
JAY, 28
JEAN LEFEVRE, 106
JEFFERIES, 140
JEFFERS, 140
JEFFERSON, 11 140
JEFFERY, 140
JEFFREY, 6 140
JEFFRIES, 140
JEFFROL, 140
JEHAN DE SMET, 106
JENNER, 69
JENNISON, 129
JEPHSON, 140
JESTER, 69
JEWELL, 81
JEWETT, 28
JIMINEZ, 147
JINDRICH, 139
JOFAN SMIRJO, 106
JOFRE, 140
JOHAN SMED, 106
JOHANN SCHMIDT, 106
JOHANNES SMID, 106

183

JOHNSON, 14
JOINER, 102
JONCOCK, 22
JORDAN, 6
JOSS, 116 118
JOSSE, 116 118
JOURDAIN, 6
JUAN HERRARA, 106
JUAN HERRERA, 106
JULIUS CAESAR, 2
JUSSI SEPPANEN, 106
KAISER, 28
KARAS, 42
KATARZYNA, 135
KATERINA, 135
KATESON, 129
KATHAROS, 134
KATHERINE, 134
KATI, 135
KATINKA, 135
KATKA, 135
KATRINA, 135
KAVANAUGH, 50
KEALEY, 50 51
KEELER, 102
KEELEY, 50 51
KEEN, 28
KEIR, 51
KELLOGG, 28
KELLY, 29
KENNEDY, 1 51
KET THE TROLL, 39
KETCHEN, 64 69 70
KETCHER, 78 81
KICHIN, 69 70
KILLEBOLE, 94
KILROY, 51 54
KING, 29 35
KING ARTHUR, 4
KING HENRY VIII, 7
KIRBY, 156
KIRK, 152
KIRKBRIDGE, 152

KIRKBY, 152
KIRKHAM, 152
KIRKLAND, 152
KIRKPATRICK, 152
KIRKWOOD, 152
KISER, 29
KITCHENER, 69 70
KITCHING, 69 70
KITSON, 129
KLASSE, 143
KLAUS, 144
KNIFESMITH, 105
KNIGHT, 70 127
KNOTT, 5
KNOWLES, 5
KYRIAKOS, 148
KYSER, 29
KYTE, 51
LA BLANC, iv
LADD, 51
LAING, 52
LAMB, 29 120
LAMBDEN, 120
LAMBE, 29
LAMBERT, 120
LAMBEY, 29
LAMBIE, 29
LAMBKIN, 29
LAMBTON, 120
LAMDEN, 29
LAMKIN, 120
LANDER, 122
LANDERS, 122
LANDRY, 14 122
LANG, 52
LANGAN, 52
LANGE, 52
LANGEMORE, 9
LANGLEY, 29
LARDNER, 70 75
LARIMER, 70 71
LARK, 29
LARKIN, 141

185

MOREAU, 42

MORENA, 42

MORGAN, 30

MORLA, 143

MORRELL, 42 53

MORRICE, 42 53

MORRILL, 42 53

MORRIN, 42 53

MORRIS, 42 53

MORRISON, 42 53

MORSE, 53

MOXON, 130

MOYLAN, 53

MOYLAND, 53

MUCKLEJOHN, iv v

MUIR, 1

MULLINS, 9

MUNDY, 30

MUNN, 53

MURIEL, 128

MURPHY, 30

MUSTANEN, 42

NAATJE, 133

NAHILL, 31

NAILSMITH, 105

NANCY, 132

NANETT, 133

NANI, 133

NAPIER, 72

NAYLOR, 103

NAYSMITH, 103

NEAL, 31

NEALE, 31

NEAVE, 30 31

NEDLER, 103

NEIL, 30

NEILD, 31

NEILL, 30

NEILS, 31

NEILSON, 31

NELLIGAN, 31

NELLIS, 31

NELLISON, 130

NELSON, 31 130

NETTER, 103

NEWBURG, 156

NEWCOMB, 31

NEWHALL, 72

NEWMAN, 17 31

NEYLAN, 31

NIALL, 30

NICHOL, 143

NICHOLAS, 135 143 144

NICHOLL, 143

NICHOLSON, 135 143

NICKERSON, 143

NICKLAS, 143

NICKLES, 143

NICKLOUS, 143

NICOLAO, 144

NICOLAUS, 144

NICOLO, 144

NIEL, 31

NIEVE, 30 31

NIEVES, 30 31

NIGEL, 31

NIHALL, 31

NIHILL, 31

NIKLAAS, 144

NIKLAS, 144

NIKOLAI, 144

NIKOLAUS, 144

NILAND, 31

NILS, 144

NINETTA, 133

NIVEN, 31

NIVIN, 31

NIVINS, 31

NIXON, 143

NOAH, 31

NOE, 31

NOEL, 31 32

NORCOTT, vi

NORCUTT, 14 153

NORLAND, 154

NORMAN, 31 128

NORRIS, 6 72 154
NORTHCOTT, 14
NORTHMAN, 128
NORTHROP, 154
NORTON, 154
NORWICH, 15
NORWOOD, 154
NOURICE, 6
NOURSE, 72
NOWELL, 31 32
NUNN, 32
NUNNE, 32
O'BRIAN, 144
O'BRIEN, 144
O'BRION, 144
O'BRYAN, 144
O'BRYANT, 144
O'NEILL, 12 31
OAKFIELD, 15
OAKLAND, 16
OAKLEY, 159
OAKWOOD, 1
OLD BAT THE BANDY, 40
OLIVE, 128
ORENCZ, 141
OSBEORN, 128
OSBORNE, 5 128
OSGOOD, 128
OSGOT, 128
OSLER, 90
OSMOND, 5
OTLEY, 118
OUTHOUSE, iv v
OXFORD, 158
PACE, 33 34
PACKARD, 17 122
PACKER, 122
PADDOCK, 53
PADGETT, 72
PAGE, 72
PAGET, 72
PAINE, 33 34
PALMER, 33

PARDEE, 6 33–35
PARDEW, 33
PARKER, 115 118 119
PARKES, 118
PARKINS, 145
PARKINSON, 145
PARKISON, 145
PARKMAN, 118
PARLIN, 145
PARNELL, 145
PARROT, 53
PARRY, 139
PARSON, 33–35
PARSONS, 61
PARTRIDGE, 53
PASTOR, 72
PATTON, 90
PAYNE, 33 34
PEACE, 33 34
PEACOCK, 53
PEARCE, 145
PEARSON, 145
PEARY, 145
PECK, 91
PEDERSSEN, 146
PEER, 145
PEPPER, 88 91
PEPPERMAN, 88 91
PER DIEU, 6
PERDUE, 33 34
PERDY, 33 34
PEREZ, 146
PERK, 145
PERKIN, 40
PERKINS, 40 145
PERKINSON, 145
PERNELL, 145
PERRIE, 145
PERRIMAN, 14
PERRY, 16 139 145
PETER, 145
PETER THE QUACK, 40
PETERKIN, 145

PETERS, 145 146
PETERSON, 129 145 146
PETRESCU, 146
PETRIE, 145
PETROPOULOS, 146
PETROV, 146
PETROVICH, 146
PETROWSKI, 146
PETRUS, 145
PETTIBONE, iv v
PETTINGILL, 34
PETURSSEN, 146
PIDGEON, 34
PIER, 145
PIERCE, 145
PIERRE, iv 145
PIERS, 145
PIERSON, 145
PIGEON, 34
PIGGE, iv v 53
PILSBURY, 156
PINDER, 72
PITTMAN, 103
PITTS, 103
PLATER, 72
PLATESMITH, 105
PLOWSMITH, 105
PLUMER, 91
PLUMMER, 91 103
PLUNKETT, 123
POETERSOHN, 146
POLLY, 142
POOLE, 1
POPE, 33 34
POPEJOY, iv v
PORTER, 6 73
PORTIER, 6
PORTMAN, 73
POTSMITH, 105
POTTER, 73 91
POTTIKER, 91
POTTINGER, 73
POTTS, 91

POUND, 81
POWERS, 34
PRATT, 34
PRENTICE, 91
PRENTISS, 91
PRESBERRY, 156 159
PRESBY, 159
PRESCOTT, vi 14 157 159
PRESLEY, 159
PRESSMAN, 16
PRESTBURY, 159
PRESTON, 159 160
PRESTWICK, 159
PRESTWOOD, 159
PRETTYMAN, 20
PRICHARD, 146
PRIDE, 35
PRIEST, 9 33 35
PRIGGMOUTH, 20
PRINCE, 35
PRIOR, 81
PRITCHARD, 147
PROPERJOHN, iv v
PROPHET, 35
PRYDE, 35
PRYOR, 81
PUDDING, 20
PULLIAM, 149
PURDUE, 6 33 35
PURDY, 33 35
QUARRELL, 62 73
QUARRIE, 92 107
QUARRIEY, 92 107
QUAYLE, 35
QUIGLEY, 54
QUINT, iv v
RAGBOTTOM, v
RAGNOR, 128
RALEIGH, 17 159
RALPH, 13 128
RAMSBOTTOM, v
RAMSDALE, 120
RAMSDEN, 120

SAYER, 104
SAYERS, 104
SAYLOR, 104
SCHERER, 123
SCRIBNER, 96 104
SCRIPPS, 54
SCYTHESMITH, 105
SEAGRAM, 5
SEALEY, 35
SEAMAN, 104
SEAMARK, 6
SEAMER, 59
SEAMSTER, 59
SEAN GOFF, 106
SEAN GOUGH, 106
SEARS, 104
SEAWARD, 128
SECKER, 5
SEELEY, 35
SEMON, 147
SEMPER, 6
SEMPLE, 6
SENYUSHKA, 147
SEWELL, 128
SEXTON, 81
SEYERS, 104
SEYMOUR, 6
SHAKELOCK, 94
SHAPCOT, 120
SHAPELL, 120
SHAPEY, 120
SHAPTON, 120
SHARMAN, 123
SHARP, 36
SHARPE, 36
SHAW, 1
SHEARER, 123 124
SHEARS, 123
SHEARSMITH, 123
SHEPARD, 123
SHEPARDSON, 123
SHEPER, 123
SHEPERD, 1

SHEPEWASSH, 20
SHEPHARD, 123
SHEPHERD, 120 123
SHEPLEY, 16 120
SHEPPERSON, 123
SHERMAN, 123
SHERWIN, 81 90 92
SHERWOOD, 162
SHIELDS, 74
SHIMKUS, 147
SHIMON, 147
SHINNER, 104
SHIPLEY, 120
SHIPMAN, 104 120
SHIPPERSON, 123
SHOEMAKER, 104
SHOESMITH, 105
SHURMAN, 124
SIBSON, 130
SIDEBOTTOM, v
SIDNEY, 6
SIENKIEWICZ, 147
SIEWAERD, 128
SIGEWEALD, 128
SILVERSMITH, 105
SIMCOCK, 147
SIMCOX, 147
SIMEON, 147
SIMEONE, 147
SIMKIN, 40
SIMKINS, 40 147
SIMMENS, 147
SIMMOND, 147
SIMMONDS, 147
SIMMONS, 147
SIMMS, 147
SIMMUNDS, 147
SIMON, 147
SIMONS, 147
SIMONSON, 147
SIMPKINS, 147
SIMPKINSON, 147
SIMPSON, 147

191

SIMS, 147
SIMSON, 147
SINCLAIR, 6
SINYARD, iv v
SIR ECHO OF THE HAELIP, 40
SIR RICHARD MALBETE, 40
SKINNER, 104
SLATER, 104
SLAUGHTER, 93
SLAYMAKER, 94
SMART, 36
SMITH, 83 97 102 105-107
SMITHE, 106 107
SMOLLETT, 16 54
SMYTH, 106 107
SMYTHE, 106 107
SNELLING, 36
SNOW, 36 55 56
SORRELL, 43 55
SOULE, 9
SPARKES, 36
SPEAR, 75 76
SPEARSMITH, 105
SPENCER, 12 75
SPICER, 93
SPIER, 75
SPINNER, 59
SPINSTER, 59
SPRAGUE, 36
SPRATT, 55
SPRIGGS, 19
SPRINGER, 36
SQUIRE, 82
ST AUBIN, 6
ST CLAIR, 6
ST DENIS, 6
ST MARK, 6
ST MAUR, 6
ST PAUL, 6
ST PIERRE, 6

STAGG, 154
STANBOROUGH, 156
STANDISH, 9
STANLAI, 10
STANLAY, 10
STANLEY, 10
STEADMAN, 119
STEARNS, 55
STEDMAN, 119
STEELE, 107
STEPTOE, iv v
STERN, 55
STERNE, 55
STEWARD, 75
STODDARD, 119
STONE, 107
STONEMAN, 107
STORY, 9
STRANG, 55
STRANGE, 36
STUART, 75
SUDBERRY, 153
SUDLOW, 153
SUNDAY, 36
SUTHERLAND, 153
SUTTON, 153
SWAIN, 82
SWAN, 154
SWARTZ, 42
SWETEMOUTH, 20
SWIFT, 55
SWINBROOK, 160
SWINBURNE, 159
SWINDELL, 14 160
SWINNARD, 17 160
SWINTON, 160
SWORDSMITH, 105
SYME, 147
SYMES, 147
SYMINGTON , 147
SYMMES, 147
SYMMONS, 147
SYMONDS, 147

SZYMANSKI, 147
TABER, 36
TABOR, 36
TADLIS, 135
TAFFY, 135
TAILLEUR, 6
TAIT, 55
TALMADGE, 36
TAMBLIN, 148
TAMBLYN, 148
TAMES, 148
TAMKIN, 148
TAMLYN, 148
TAMMAS, 148
TAMP, 148
TAMPLIN, 148
TANNER, 107
TATE, 55
TAVENER, 90
TAVERNER, 93
TAVIS, 136
TAYLOR, 1 6 83 107
TEMPLE, 36
TESSLER, 124
THATCHER, 92 94 107
THOMA, 148
THOMAS, 128 148
THOMASSON, 148
THOME, 148
THOMPKINS, 148
THOMPKINSON, 148
THOMPSON, 9 148
THOMSEN, 148
THURSTAN, 128
THURSTON, 128
TIFFANY, 36
TILLER, 119
TILLEY, 9
TILLMAN, 119
TILLOTSON, 130
TINKER, 9 107
TOBIN, 6
TODD, 37

TOLER, 108
TOLLER, 108
TOLLMAN, 14 108
TOLMAN, 108
TOLSON, 148
TOM, 148
TOMAN, 148
TOMAS, 148
TOMASO, 148
TOMBLIN, 148
TOMCZAK, 148
TOMKIN, 40
TOMKINS, 40
TOMLINSON, 148
TOMMY, 148
TOMMY ANN, 148
TOMMY JO, 148
TOMPKINS, 148
TOMPKINSON, 148
TOMPSON, 148
TOMSDOGTHER, 2
TOMSETT, 148
TOMSON, 148
TOPP, 55
TOPPER, 55
TOWLE, 108
TOWLER, 108
TOWNSEND, 14
TRAPP, 108
TRAPPE, 108
TRAVES, 108
TRAVIS, 108
TREVORE, 9
TRIPP, 37
TRIPPER, 37
TROTTER, 75 90 94
TROUT, 75
TROUTMAN, 75
TRUMAN, 1 37
TUBBS, 99 108
TUBMAN, 61 99 108
TUCKER, 1 124
TUNNEY, 37

194

WHITFIELD, 118 155
WHITLOCK, 56
WHITLOW, 155
WHITLY, 155
WHITMAN, 56
WHITMERE, 156
WHITMORE, 156
WHITNEY, 156
WHITSET, 56
WHITSON, 56
WHITT, 56
WHITTED, 56
WHITTEN, 56 155
WHITTIER, 109 155
WHITTINGTON, 156
WHYTE, 56
WHYTERE, 109
WIDDOWSON, 38
WIGBEORN, 128
WIGFRIP, 4
WILCOCK, 22 150
WILCOX, 22 150
WILDE, 38
WILDER, 9 38
WILHELM, 150
WILKES, 150
WILKIE, 150
WILKINS, 150
WILKINSON, 150
WILL SCARLET, 39
WILLAHELM, 149
WILLARD, 128
WILLCOCK, 150
WILLE, 150
WILLEM, 150
WILLETS, 150
WILLETT, 150
WILLIAM, 13 128 149
WILLIAM THE CONQUEROR, 1
WILLIAMS, 6 150
WILLIAMSON, 149
WILLIS, 150

WILLMETT, 150
WILLS, 150
WILLSDOGTHER, 2
WILLSON, 150
WILSON, 14 150
WINNE, 56
WINSLOW, 9
WINTER, 38
WINTERBOTTOM, v
WINTERS, 38
WISE, 38
WISEMAN, 38
WISHARD, 38
WISMAN, 38
WITHERS, 120 125
WITTE, 56
WITTMAN, 56
WOLSEY, 128
WONTER, 94
WOOD, 1
WOODARD, 119 120 162
WOODBRIDGE, 162
WOODBURY, 156
WOODFALL, 163
WOODFORD, 163
WOODGATE, 119
WOODHEAD, 163
WOODMAN, 119 120
WOODRIDGE, 163
WOODRUFF, 120
WOODS, 119 120 151
WOODWARD, 119 120
WOOLF, 5
WOOLFOLK, 125
WOOLFORD, 128
WOOLMAN, 1 125
WREN, 38
WRENN, 38
WRIGHT, 83
WRIGLEY, 159
WULFGIFU, 4
WULFSIGE, 128
WULFSTAN, 4